What others have said about PATIENT-DIRECTED DYING:

"Tom Preston is the doctor we would all wish to have at our bedside as we face the final days of life: compassionate, wise, and kind. He believes that each patient knows what constitutes quality of life for herself, knows what is endurable and what is not, and knows if and when patient-directed dying is appropriate. This book is for all of us—it's sane, helpful, thoughtful, and reassuring."

—Susan Dunshee
Board of Directors
Compassion & Choices

"After a lifetime of practice and well over a decade of compassionate involvement in providing information and support to terminally ill patients, Tom Preston has provided us with rational arguments in favor of having a law that permits terminally ill patients to hasten their own dying processes. This book is a must for patients who want choice in dying."

—Dr. Richard MacDonald

"This volume outlines the key issues in the right-to-die debate in a way that will inform readers and should reframe the topic. Dr. Preston's book on death with dignity combines his decades of medical experience with the insights of a non-judgmental human being who has sincerely listened to the preferences of dying patients. Those who have personally witnessed the trials of terminally ill people, or who are trying to make up their minds on this public issue, will be grateful for his perspective."

—Rev Ralph Mero
Unitarian Universalist Minister
Boston MA

Patient-Directed Dying

Other books by Tom Preston, M.D.

"Coronary Artery Surgery: A Critical Review."
Raven Press: New York, 1977

"The Clay Pedestal."
Madrona Press: Seattle, 1981; Scribners' Paperback, 1986

"Final Victory, Taking Charge of the Last Stages of Life."
Forum, Prima Publishing, Roseville, CA, September, 2000.

Few physicians are willing to discuss and openly endorse patient-directed aid in dying, but Dr. Preston changes all that in this timely and insightful volume. He clearly articulates that death is a topic that needs to become both public and personal, and that it transcends beliefs or stereotypes. His trailblazing discussion of the need for patient-directed control over dying grips the reader from beginning to end. It won't kill you to buy this book, but you may someday die a lot better because you did.

—*Paul A. Spiers, Ph.D.*
Chairman, Board of Directors, AUTONOMY, Inc.
Board of Directors,
Compassion & Choices

With its focus on "patient-directed dying" this is an informative and deeply moving book that should be read by everyone interested in "how we die today." Dr Preston is a cardiologist who has been a recognized authority in the Right-To-Die movement for 15 years, and writes with extraordinary sensitivity and concern about his experiences in working with dying patients.

—Midge Levy, ACSW, Co-President,
Compassion & Choices of Washington

PATIENT-DIRECTED DYING

A CALL FOR LEGALIZED AID IN DYING FOR THE TERMINALLY ILL

TOM PRESTON, M.D.

iUniverse Star
New York Lincoln Shanghai

PATIENT-DIRECTED DYING
A CALL FOR LEGALIZED AID IN DYING FOR THE TERMINALLY ILL

Copyright © 2006, 2007 by Thomas A. Preston

All rights reserved. No part of this book may be used or reproduced by any means, graphic, electronic, or mechanical, including photocopying, recording, taping or by any information storage retrieval system without the written permission of the publisher except in the case of brief quotations embodied in critical articles and reviews.

iUniverse Star
an iUniverse, Inc. imprint

iUniverse books may be ordered through booksellers or by contacting:

iUniverse
2021 Pine Lake Road, Suite 100
Lincoln, NE 68512
www.iuniverse.com
1-800-Authors (1-800-288-4677)

The information, ideas, and suggestions in this book are not intended as a substitute for professional medical advice. Before following any suggestions contained in this book, you should consult your personal physician. Neither the author nor the publisher shall be liable or responsible for any loss or damage allegedly arising as a consequence of your use or application of any information or suggestions in this book.

ISBN-13: 978-1-58348-461-6 (pbk)
ISBN-13: 978-0-595-87751-5 (ebk)
ISBN-10: 1-58348-461-2 (pbk)
ISBN-10: 0-595-87751-6 (ebk)

Printed in the United States of America

To the many who, while they were dying, taught me with love, courage, and dignity.

ACKNOWLEDGMENTS

The first serious acknowledgment I must make is my inability to recall all who helped me in the writing of this book. During the more than seven years this project has been in the making I have asked for and received help and suggestions from many friends and colleagues, and I ask forgiveness for those I fail to mention.

I am deeply indebted to my editor, Phyllis Hatfield, who prodded me to escape from the essay format that she calls "doctor dreary," in reference to the sort of writing one might find in a medical journal. Kristen Kennell, similarly urged me to find a style that "everyone can read." The support and advice of these two colleagues led me to develop the dialogue format I have adopted.

I am grateful to those who have helped in directing and editing the manuscript: Sheila Cook, Judith Gordon, Karl and Shirley Ingebritsen, Ralph Mero, Ted Preston, Timothy Quill, Ronaldo Rubin, and Paul Spiers. I am indebted to Susan Dunshee, Assen Nicolov, Kathryn Tucker, Jim Werth, and Dr. Dick MacDonald for their encouragement and support. I also want to thank Margaret P. Battin and Charles

Acknowledgments

McKhann for having written books that greatly influenced and aided me in writing this one, and Barbara Witt for her technical support, including the cover.

Lastly, as any writer knows, home support is critical. I thank Molly, Stephanie, and Hilary for tolerating comments and discussions about a subject uneasy for anyone not engrossed in it.

CONTENTS

Preface xv

PART I **The Trials of Dying**
Chapter 1 As Mom Lay Dying 3

PART II **The Quest for Patient-Directed Dying**
Chapter 2 "Doc, I Don't Want to Die That Way"
—The Story of John 15
Chapter 3 Dying My Way
—The Story of Marcia 41
Chapter 4 When Ideology Trumps Compassion
—The Story of Michael 61
Chapter 5 Who Decides?
—The Story of Agnes 87

PART III **Going Forward**
Chapter 6 Going Forward 115
Mercy Doesn't Kill 115
Supremely Backward 120
The Turning Point—Terminal Illness 122

Contents

Who's Dying, Anyway? 124
Privatize Dying! 127
The Future of Dying 134

Appendix   The Oregon Death with Dignity Act
           (DWDA) 139
Glossary..143
Readings 149
Explanatory Notes 155
Index 173

The wise man will live as long as he ought,
But not as long as he can.
—Seneca

It is not physician-assisted suicide that poses the greatest threat to the poor and the disabled but physician-assisted eternal life.
—Garret Keizer[1]

My deepest desire is always to choose death with dignity over a life that has become either hopelessly painful and dysfunctional or empty and devoid of all meaning. That is the only way I know that would allow me to honor the God in whose image I believe I was created.
—Bishop John Shelby Spong[2]

PATIENT-DIRECTED DYING

PREFACE

The suffering of dying patients frequently dismayed me during nearly 40 years of active medical practice. I knew that some suffering while dying was inevitable, but what bothered me most was the hand of my physician colleagues and their medical technology in extending the suffering. Who among us has not watched a parent, sibling, or child linger needlessly in physical or emotional anguish while the descendants of Hippocrates and Galen postpone inescapable death until the final cell of life is spent?

I will never gainsay the wonderful advances of modern preventive and curative medicine, which have given virtually all of us extended useful and meaningful life. We have applied imaginative and reasoned creativity to this accomplishment. But by blocking efforts to help dying patients in their quest for quicker, more peaceful dying, we defer to irrational fears and the intransigence of ideology and tradition. Society's refusal to help terminally ill patients die is a failure to adapt to modern medical methods. It is a failure of human responsibility for what humans have created.

I believe that much of the resistance of physicians, jurists, and the lay public to physician aid in dying comes from not understanding—or in the case of physicians, not acknowledging—how we die today. It is prudent to talk about dying and to prepare for it. To attempt to denigrate aid in dying as part of a "culture of death" is to deny death rather than to accept it as a meaningful end of earthly existence.

The very purpose of modern medicine is to prevent natural dying, and very few of us alive now will die naturally. Dying is a process that for most people starts with the onset of an ultimately fatal illness, and progresses through many stages. The process of dying includes innumerable medical interventions that range in complexity from swallowing an aspirin to receiving an organ transplant or gene therapy.

Death is not an isolated event at the last moment of life; it is the culmination of the medically managed process of dying. We have preempted nature; we have "played God" with our artificial extensions of life. To decide *how* to die is playing God no more than is deciding how to *prevent* natural death. We defer death to a time when someone—physician, spouse, patient—must make a decision about how to end life. The central question of how we die is: *Who makes the decision?* Why do we not allow the dying person to make the decision?

The movement for physician aid in dying has long been hampered by the term physician-assisted "suicide." Although linguistically correct, by time-honored usage the word "suicide" is incorrect when applied to dying patients; the term is applied appropriately only when a *non-dying* person, who has a curable or manageable condition, enacts his or her own death. A terminally ill patient has an entirely different condition. He or she is going to die soon regardless of any further intervention, and his or her condition of fatal illness is not curable or manageable. When a terminally ill patient plans and ends his or her life with the help of a physician who makes available a lethal drug or agent, it is *patient-directed aid in dying*. Because of the length of this term, I primarily use the abbreviated *aid in dying* to indicate this means of dying, in conformity with the most common usage of those who support the practice. I also use the term *patient-directed dying* interchangeably with *aid in dying*, because *patient-directed dying* more accurately orients the reader to who is instituting and controlling the act, and therefore is a more accurate description of it. Please refer to the glossary for this and other related terms.

As a society we have distorted the ancient principle of the sanctity of life to include all technological transformations of human life, however harmful they may be. We must sanctify or respect life to its natural end, but when we use medical technology to extend lives beyond their natural ends we must be careful of what we sanctify. We are in danger of sanctifying unnaturally created biological existence rather than meaningful human life. We must remember to sanctify death as the natural conclusion to life.

Much of the harm to dying patients arises when physicians are unable to step back from their professional goal of saving and prolonging life in order to recognize the exigency of their equally important second duty: to relieve suffering. Physicians who use curing but not caring to the very end are the primary agents of excessive end-of-life suffering. They must unlearn the practice of withdrawing from their dying patients and replace it with the practice of limiting the harmful excesses of modern dying, and being willing to help people escape from the indignities and suffering of unnaturally prolonged dying.

I have watched and participated in the great debate over aid in dying. I was a plaintiff in the U.S. Supreme Court case *Glucksberg v. Washington,* and during the arguments before the Court I realized that the justices were relying on traditional views of suicide rather than making the distinction between patients who will die soon and people who would not otherwise die. They saw death as an isolated final act rather than as the last medical intervention in the process of dying.

I have watched as a minority of Americans leverage their fears and narrow ideologies against state legislation that would represent the majority view on this issue. I have watched as too few of my physician colleagues are willing to back their private endorsement of physician aid in dying with open medical practice, much less public advocacy. I have watched as the dominant national political power moves to insert and encase its minority view about dying as the law of the land. And I have listened as too few Americans have the will or the means to understand and act on this issue.

I have written this book in an attempt to help thoughtful and compassionate Americans become engaged in helping terminally ill patients die more humanely. We are all involved in the debate—it envelops us every time one of our loved ones, or even a not-too-well-known friend or co-worker, becomes ill and dies. When we intersect with the agents of our dying processes—physicians, hospice nurses, other medical or hospital personnel, and religious leaders, politicians, and judges—we must assert ourselves as forcefully as do those who would deny our loved ones peaceful deaths of their own choosing.

I have attempted to portray here, in the stories of five people who died, the primary issues involved in the debate for peaceful dying. The first story, my mother's, embodies many of the problems dying patients encounter, and does not involve patient-directed dying (aid in dying). The other four stories are composites of many of my patients, relating their experiences in seeking aid in dying, and my experiences with them. I have changed many of the characteristics and conditions of all four of them in order to protect their identities. They are examples only, and are not meant to be statistically representative of those patients who seek patient-directed aid in dying.

I hope their experiences will show you how hard an individual must work if he or she is to die peacefully today, and will inspire you to work toward changing public understanding and the laws. If we don't become involved now, others will decide how we die.

—Thomas A. Preston, M.D.

PART I

The Trials of Dying

Chapter 1

AS MOM LAY DYING[1]

It was a race to get to my 91-year-old mother's bedside before she died. In my physician's mind I anticipated her death, but I had never considered that I, and not a heart attack or stroke, would bring down her final curtain.

The phone call came from my mother's nursing home in Ohio. "Your mother is slipping," the head nurse said. These are the gently alarming but not final words we in the profession calculate to suffuse slowly into fearful and unreceptive minds. My mother had been "slipping" for months, if not years, and the measured ambiguity of the words shored my defenses. "The doctor wants to put your mother into the hospital for tests."

"No," I snapped. "She doesn't want that, and neither do I." She would be no match for faceless young physicians who had never met her and who would follow the book in ordering scans and inserting tubes to look at almost every part of her disintegrating body. And after the tests would come the harsh treatments.

---

[1] This section published first in the *Seattle Weekly*, Sept 22, 1993.

But the nurse continued. "Her kidneys have stopped working and her blood pressure has dropped to 80." Between the eyes, irrefutable. What the nurse said next came like an unannounced jab with her largest needle. "She isn't drinking, and without an IV to get liquids into her she won't make it. We know your mother will fight it, and we know how you and your brothers feel, so we won't start an IV unless you ask us to." No time for thinking, for analyzing, for consulting. "No, don't do it," I heard myself say. "Don't start an IV."

I knew my mother would die without it. A simple, "Yes, put in an IV" would have kept her alive for days, possibly weeks or months, until the humanless voices of death vanquished even the machines crowded into her room. But for the woman who conceived me, I was saying "No." Until that moment, I had imagined a battlefield: me standing between my mother, unconscious and hours from death no matter what, and a confused, wild-eyed intern intent on hooking her to a respirator. Now I battled only myself.

I desperately wanted to get to her bedside before she died, to include her one last confirming time in what I had decided.

It seems to me we start dying at puberty, boys with the rush of testosterone sludging minds and arteries to violence, women with estrogen first inciting breasts and reproductive organs, and later withdrawing with the skeletal substance of existence. My mother's dying became evident when she was in her early sixties. Her fingers began to gnarl like the knots on maple trees cut high on their trunks, and slowly it became painful for her to use her feet, hips, hands, and shoulders. With increasing inactivity the calcium fled from her thinning bones, and in her eighties she broke both hips and several vertebrae. Spurs growing from vertebrae encroached on nerves, further weakening her already wasted limbs. "Above all," she told my brothers and me on many occasions, "I don't want to be put into one of those tiny cells" in her retirement community's nursing home.

At age 81, an operation to decompress nerves in her neck left my mother much weaker, and unable to swallow large pills or chunks of food. At ages 85 and 86 she had cataract operations, the second complicated by a blinding hemorrhage and infection at the back of the eye. She had no choice; she had to go into one of those "tiny cells" she had so much dreaded.

Her mind remained facile to the end, but gradually she reached total immobility, unable to move except to bring her left arm in front of her chest, but no more. She could not eat, sit, or go to the bathroom without assistance, and she could not see well enough to watch television. But she had little pain except for her eyes, which were constantly sore and dry. She enjoyed visitors, and lived for the infrequent visits of her sons who lived in Philadelphia, Madison (Wisconsin), and Seattle.

After Dad died, Mother had made out a living will and sent it to me for comment and signature. In formal language she asked not to be kept alive through artificial means or heroic measures if she were dying. Despite my background and approval of what she was doing, I found it difficult to discuss it with her. "Look," I blurted out, "what if you have a heart attack and need machines and continuous intravenous medicines to support you? Is that all right?"

"Don't ask me that," she said. "How can I possibly answer that? You're the doctor. You're supposed to know what to do."

But her answers left no room for doubt. "I don't want to live connected to a machine," she said. "When my time comes, I want to go. Don't you let them keep me alive. It's not my way...or God's way." And she was a God-fearing person. Several years later, she named me as her decision-maker in case she could not make medical decisions for herself. She had checked the box on the form that instructed her physician to withhold even intravenous fluids if she were incurably ill and dying.

"You decide," is all she said.

In medical school, and even more so during internship and residency, I had learned by the example of my mentors that the role of the physician is to make decisions for patients. Unlike most of my peers, I have always had trouble with medical paternalism, and I naturally embraced the trend of the past 25 years of including patients in important decisions. But what's easy for physicians to do, even me, is to just choose from a menu of tests, or treatments. We were never taught that doing nothing is an option. In fact, we learned by example that doing nothing is unacceptable. Yet over the years I have learned sometimes to do nothing but provide comfort for my dying patients who wanted it that way. This was never easy for me, but often much better for them. But the hardest of all, still, is to turn off a ventilator, or stop a life-supporting medicine that hastens the death of a hopelessly ill patient. It goes against the grain of how we see ourselves as healers.

Patient-Directed Dying

At the nursing home I raced up the stairs and down hall C, the middle of five spokes fanning off the central nurses' station. Mother was there, alive and alone in her room, lying quietly in bed. Her eyes were sunken a finger's-breadth below their sockets, the fragile ridges of cheekbone covered only by a layer of tightly drawn, tissue-thin, colorless skin. Without moving her head she turned her eyes to meet me. I hugged her, almost smothered her, and wept. It was a message I hadn't intended to give. My tears beaded on her face like rain falling on parched earth.

"Mother, are you having any pain?"

"No," she said, and then, "am I dying?"

"Yes, probably," I said. She said nothing and looked the other way. We talked briefly about family, but she was too tired to keep her eyes open. Only her breathing broke the silence of the onrushing night.

Later in the evening there was a knock on the door—doors are always open in the nursing home. It was the daughter of Mother's good friend, Mildred Churchill, who lived across the hall and three rooms down in this nursing home.

"How's your mother?" I asked, slipping out into the hall.

"Not good," the daughter said, nodding toward the form slumped over in a wheelchair. "She had a stroke a month or so ago, and they took her to the hospital. She couldn't swallow, so they did an operation and put a tube into her stomach. That's how the nurses feed her, through the tube. She just got back here a week ago."

Mildred Churchill was 82 when I first met her about five years ago. I thought she was in fairly good shape then, although she couldn't walk and motored around the halls in her electric wheelchair. About a year ago Mildred began having trouble keeping food down, first solids, and then even liquids. This worsened over about six months. No pain. They took her to the hospital, where among a battery of tests they had her swallow barium, which on an X-ray shows up as it descends into the stomach. Cancer of the esophagus. Bad prognosis, 50 percent dead in eight months, but 5 to 10 percent survive five years. "The doctors were very open about the seriousness of it, but said surgery was the best chance for a cure," the daughter had told me on an earlier visit. "We're lucky to have her. You know, her heart stopped twice after the surgery, and each time they had to shock her right in bed. And then, the radiation therapy made her so sick and weak."

"To have gone through all that, your mother must have a strong will to live," I said.

"I'm not so sure, but it doesn't matter. She had no choice in it. Sometimes I wonder if it was the right thing to do."

Mildred had spent six weeks in the hospital after surgery to take out the tumor and attach the stomach to the upper esophagus. The rest of the time she endured the tests, needles, X-ray treatments, nausea, vomiting, and weakness. She had returned to the nursing home, but it was a different Mildred. Her head tilted forward and a bit to one side, and her smile drooped a little. She was thinner. But most noticeably, she didn't talk so much.

Now, standing in this nursing home hallway again with Mildred's distraught daughter, I raged inside. But perhaps, I thought, Mildred and her daughter wanted it this way. My

"I'm sorry" was barely audible, and nothing more came out. The daughter stood silently, endlessly, and then broke. Between cries she admitted, "It's not what mother would want. It's horrible, she still has her mind, although she can't speak it, and I know she's suffering in this condition. But there's nothing more to do."

"There's nothing more to do" is for the family. But for physicians there's always a lot to do—heroic and futile procedures neatly fitted into proper medical practice. Where did we take the turn down the unforked, dead-end road that says we must stand by and watch while doctors do something for every medical condition, however much misery it may produce? What is this process, uncontrolled after the first step, with ends and means no longer the choosing of the person who suffers them? Is this the drowning man clutching at any rope, or perhaps the misguided counsel of loved ones who cannot let go?

Or have doctors so acclimated us to what they do that we unknowingly surrender choice, enfeebled and frightened, after we first supplicate them? Where do the elderly, the dying, lose their grip on themselves, on their power to steer their own ships, to die naturally as persons and in peace, unassaulted by the imperatives of tearless technology? Why do the sons and daughters of Hippocrates stand silently outside our mothers' rooms peering at flashing numbers while writing orders for more dripping medicines to shore up collapsed veins and souls? Why, before committing their patients to the treacherous rapids of terminal therapy, don't they ask one simple question: "What do you want?" Why don't the doctors at least give each patient, like Barney Clark had, a key to turn off the machines?

I took leave of Mildred's daughter in the hallway and reentered my mother's room very quietly. Her course was now irrevocable. Her kidneys had "shut down," she was bleeding internally, and her blood pressure was almost undetectable. She was too weak to talk, except for one exchange. She tried to move her left arm, the "good one," and groaned as she seemed to point to her chest. I asked if it hurt, and I think she said "Yes," but I wasn't sure. I asked the nurses, unfailingly supportive, to give Mother a painkiller. They agreed and quickly did. Within 15 minutes Mother's gaze was fixed and she moved only in breathing. I would never have her confirmation of my decision. She died four hours later, nine hours after I had arrived. As I stood beside her bed, with her lifeless hand in mine, my pounding heart grew calm.

Three months later Mildred's daughter phoned to say her mother had finally died. After countless visits, sitting silently with her mother who drooled constantly and groaned occasionally, the daughter conferred with family members, and together they asked the staff to stop tube-feeding Mildred. Mildred had no living will or advance written directive, and after much discussion the family's wish was officially denied. But the staff reduced the amount and frequency of the feedings. Three weeks later, nine months after her operation, Mildred Churchill died.

Although I will always be nagged by the thought that I pulled the trigger on my mother, I know what I did was right for her. I had saved Mother a lot of suffering when she had no life to live, and if it was hard to do, it's because it is contrary to the traditions of a society too slow to make medical technology serve people, not diseases and professional habits. But my unease about relieving my mother of needless suffering is nothing compared to the abiding distress of Mildred Churchill's daughter and millions of others who forever feel responsible for doing nothing while professionals prolonged the painful dying of their loved ones. If physicians will not learn to care as well as they cure, we sons and daughters must take control to guide our dying elders through their final passages.

PART II

The Quest for Patient-Directed Dying

CHAPTER 2

"DOC, I DON'T WANT TO DIE THAT WAY"—THE STORY OF JOHN

I knew John was dying. When I first met him he was sitting up in bed in his room at home, and he looked me straight in the eye and said, "Doc, I can't keep going this way for another three or four months. I need to end it."

John H. wasn't my patient, but I was seeing him to help a distraught physician-friend, Dr. Z, who had hailed me the day before in the hospital corridor. "What do you do when your patient wants you to help him die?" Dr. Z had asked me.

As I pondered my reply, he quickly unloaded his burden. "I don't know how to handle it," he said. "I'd like to help him, but I'm not ready to do this. I have nothing against his ending his life; it's just that I can't do it for him."

It was the quintessential physician's reply to a patient's plea for release from the agony of dying. Dr. Z knew there were no more medical magic bullets, no more ways to beat the cancer that began 18 months ago in John's lungs and was now spreading in his brain. As Dr. Z said, there's "nothing more I can do," and his distress showed in his face and his fidgety hands and his stooped shoulders. Dr. Z was, as he said, "not prepared" to handle his patient's request for help in dying.

"Doc, I Don't Want to Die that Way"—The Story of John

Dr. Z's patients raved about how he cared about them so much, and it was easy to see why. About 55 years old, he had been a family-practice physician for 28 years, and he was an easygoing, moderately extroverted man, with the best-known laugh in the doctors' lounge. He had carried his affability to the medical school dissection table and then to the hospital bedside where he had a way of making seriously sick patients smile. But he was too laid-back to advance professionally. He never aspired to be Chief of Staff, or medical director of his clinic, or even chairman of one of the many hospital committees. Nor did he aspire to dress well, although he never looked sloppy.

I had seen him talking to patients in the hallway many times over the past dozen or so years, and the secret of his success seemed obvious to me: he never talked down to a patient, he hugged his women patients, patted his men patients on the shoulder, and always asked his patients how their children were doing.

But now Dr. Z couldn't cope with a request that cut through the hardened skin of his comfort zone. He wanted to help John H., but he was floundering in seas uncharted by the architects of medical education: neither his training nor sensibility gave him guidance.

"What am I supposed to do?" he said looking off into the distance. "He's had two courses of chemotherapy after surgery to take out the primary tumor, but now he refuses any more. I want to help him, but he won't let me. And I can't do what he wants me to do." He then looked straight at me and said, "What would you do?"

"I'd go talk to him," I said almost reflexively.

"Would you? Really? Will you do that for me?"

"Well…yes, I will, but I'll just talk to him. I won't be his doctor in any way—what you do about his request will still be your job."

"Okay, I understand. And thanks."

Dr. Z had caught me. I would make a house call to a patient I hadn't before met.

Among the many sad aspects of meeting dying patients for the first time is not having known them before they became terminally ill—when they were fully involved with life and the people around them, the way they were for most of their lives. Their character remains the same, and is often a source of joy for everyone around them, but the process of dying consumes patients' spirits as well as their bodies.

John H. looked up with a faint smile when his wife Else led me into his room. He was 73, a retired high school health and social studies teacher. He was obviously wasted physically, his face gaunt beneath the unshaven stubble. He welcomed me courteously with a half-extended hand barely more than flaccid. John had lost about 40 pounds in the last year and a half, Else had told me.

After an appropriate period of introducing ourselves to each other I said: "Dr. Z tells me you've pretty much had it and are thinking of leaving us." (I maintained the taboo against the "D" word by this euphemism.) "Why do you want to end your life now?"

"Doc, I Don't Want to Die that Way"—The Story of John

"It's not that I want to die," John said. "It's just that living the way I am now is not worth it." He paused and then added, "And you know, it's going to get worse."

"Is it pain?" I asked.

"Doc, I can handle the pain. I'm wearing these patches on my skin and they're doing a pretty good job. I mean, I do get pain, but I can control it." John took a few labored breaths and then continued, "But it's spread to my brain now, and they say it's just a matter of time before the cancer pushes so hard against my brain I'll have convulsions or become unconscious."

"But you're in good hands here at home, aren't you? You'll be well taken care of, won't you?" John was in the house that he and Else had bought 18 years ago. "And, if you become unconscious as they say you might, you won't feel anything, so you won't suffer."

"Doc, that's not it," he shot back quickly. "I don't want to die that way, lying here 'out of it' for weeks, or even if it's just a few days. I don't want people seeing me that way."

"I understand how you feel, John, and I know it would be hard on your wife, but I'll bet she wouldn't mind taking care of you whatever condition you're in. And you're better off here at home than in a hospital or nursing home, don't you think?"

"Oh sure, she or whoever's helping her will take good care of me, I know that, but …" and he hesitated. "Look, I know they'll do anything for me, but I don't want to have to be taken care of that way. Do you know I have a catheter in my bladder, and now I don't always know when my bowels are moving and sometimes I soil the bed before someone can lift me onto the bedside commode? And then my wife or the aide has to clean it up. And what happens after I'm unconscious? Does everyone just sit and look at me all day?"

I knew that John was defining his existence after what he considered meaningful life had ended for him. "What's the purpose in it all?" he continued. "Why do I have to lie here and rot away until I'm nothing but skin and bones and the tumor pushes my eyeballs out of their sockets? Or they put me on a breathing machine? No thanks. I don't want to go through all that, and I don't want my family to have to go through it, either. Enough's enough. I've put up the good fight. Now it's time to end it."

Many dying patients I have known feel the way John described it: they don't want to die, but knowing that they will be dead within a few weeks or months, they don't want to continue living a mere physical, biological existence. *They aren't choosing death over life: they know they're going to die, and they're choosing how and when to do it.* They're choosing to end a life that has become unduly burdensome for themselves and their loved ones.

Like John, patients who wish to direct their dying usually aren't suffering uncontrolled pain. Only about 15 percent of them rank pain avoidance as their major reason for hastening death.[3] Good pain control, or medical palliative care (also called "comfort care"), can control symptoms and allow peaceful dying for the majority of dying patients. But even with good palliative care directed by a hospice team, as many as 35 percent of patients report their pain during the last week of life as severe or intolerable, and 35 percent report their shortness of breath as unbearable.[4]

In addition, many patients suffer physical symptoms other than pain—e.g., shortness of breath, nausea, vomiting, diarrhea, extreme weakness and fatigue, or loss of bowel and bladder control—for which palliative care is less effective.[5] It is hard for most of us to appreciate the overwhelming fatigue many patients experience while dying. And while morphine and other drugs can stop pain, they often have bothersome side effects of their own, especially extreme constipation or unwanted sedation.

"As I've told you, I don't believe in unnecessary suffering," John said. "I'm willing to put up with side effects of treatments so long as there's a chance of beating or controlling my cancer, but when there's no more chance of stopping it, I don't see the sense of just putting in time until I die. I can't see any good to come of suffering that'll be hard on my family and me. I don't think it's right—it's not my way."

People have varying views and beliefs on whether or how much they should accept suffering. Many patients accept suffering during life or at death as an expression of God's will. For example, when anesthesia became available for childbirth in the nineteenth century, many people opposed it for violating the biblical command: *In sorrow thou shalt bring forth children.* Suffering, they argued, is part of God's will.[6] The dispute over anesthesia in childbirth continued until Queen Victoria accepted chloroform when she delivered her eighth child, on April 7, 1853. Similarly, some people believe that suffering is a natural part of dying that prepares the soul for the afterlife, or is necessary for redemption.

Like many Americans, John does not share this view. He does not find spiritual value in suffering. To him and many others, dying is hard enough, and they don't want to suffer just because others believe it is necessary or good for them. If you do not find spiritual reward in suffering, it is legitimate and reasonable to minimize it at the end of life.

Patients like John commonly cite nonphysical problems as reasons for wanting to die: poor quality of life ("life is not worth living"), loss of control, not wanting to burden others, and a "readiness to die." For these dying patients suffering is primarily existential, not physical—they don't want to live beyond the point when life has no meaning for them.

For many people dying is a threat to their integrity and to their sense of purpose in life. They don't want to draw out their disability to the point where all they can do before death finally comes is to lie in bed all day, exposed to the cruel vicissitudes of physical decomposition. Dying can strip a person of the qualities they most esteem in themselves and that make them unique to others. How these persons die is important to them—they don't want to fester physically and emotionally while obligating their loved ones to care for them. For them, dying is not a welcome bedmate.

These "existential" reasons for wanting to die reflect a dying patient's beliefs and values acquired over a lifetime. Spiritually, they suffer while entrapped for weeks or months in an existence that lacks purpose or meaning for them.

"Doc, I Don't Want to Die that Way"—The Story of John

Society causes them real harm by preventing them from escaping spiritual suffering.

No dying patient should go without good palliative care, but, unfortunately, good palliative care is not sufficient for all dying patients.

I wanted to let John know I was sympathetic and wasn't there to tell him what he should do, or that he shouldn't want to die. I told him I was just trying to understand how he had come to his decision to die before it was absolutely necessary, because this decision is complex and never easy for anyone, and should be void of treatable causes. John sounded determined and rational, but I wondered if he had issues that he wasn't getting out.

I turned to Else who was standing at the foot of the bed, arms limp at her sides, listening attentively but not commenting on what her husband was saying. "What do you think, Else? How do you feel about John dying sooner than absolutely necessary?"

A small woman, Else looked to be younger than John, at most 65 years old, though her hair was almost entirely white. She answered me slowly and softly.

"I want John to do what he thinks best, and if he needs to die soon I won't try to stop him. Mostly, I don't want him to suffer at the end," she trailed off, looking at me as though she had more to say.

I waited five, maybe ten seconds, and she went on: "It's just that I don't like the idea of him committing suicide."

Patient-Directed Dying

"What's the difference?" John snapped. What does it matter if they keep me alive another two months or I die now? I don't care what you call it. When you get to where I am, I don't see it as suicide. It's dying sooner rather than later, so I won't have to lie here in misery for two more months. There's nothing wrong with it."

John looked away from both of us. "I don't know why I can't die the way I want to do it," he said, almost whispering. "Why should other people push their moralities on me and be able to say I can't die peacefully, my way?"

"I think basically we're with you, John," I said. "I don't think Else is saying it's wrong. It's just natural she should worry about you doing something we've been told all our lives is wrong."

Quickening his speech, John said, "But suicide is when you don't have to die. That's what's wrong with it. We don't want people dying when they don't have to. But when you have a fatal disease and there's no treatment except something that may string it out a few more weeks or months, and you're going to die anyway, what difference does it make if you end the suffering, if it's what you really want to do?"

John was right. A terminally ill patient who requests and then takes a prescribed lethal dose of medicine is not committing suicide in the common, ordinary, and traditional sense of suicide—for two reasons. First, a person who commits common and ordinary suicide has a condition that is reversible or potentially so, or can be treated and improved. On the other hand, a terminally ill[7] patient has a problem that is not reversible and cannot be overcome with time, nor can it be treated medically and improved long term.

Second, a person who commits suicide triggers the dying process; he does not have to die. Were it not for the suicidal act, the person would live. In contrast, a terminally ill patient who asks for medicine to help him die does not initiate the dying process—it is already underway—and although the dying process can be modified, the death itself can't be prevented. The distinction between persons who commit suicide and dying patients lies in their fundamentally different conditions. For a terminally ill person who is suffering, dying can be a rational response to a condition that is not temporary and will not go away.

The expression "physician-assisted suicide" is inaccurate and misleading when applied to a terminally ill and *dying* patient who directs his or her death with the help of a physician. It is not suicide. Nor is this book about suicide. It is about *aid in dying*, or *patient-directed dying*, the terms I use throughout this book for the specific act of a terminally ill patient ending his life. Rarely I use the euphemistic terms "hastened dying" or "hastened death" to mean the same thing.

In aid in dying, the patient—not a doctor or a team of health-care providers—*directs* the time and means of death. And a physician who prescribes a lethal amount of medicine for a terminally ill patient has not assisted in a suicide if and when the patient voluntarily takes the medicine to end his life; the physician has *enabled* a dying patient to die on his own terms rather than by medically set terms. The patient directs the dying; the physician enables it. Truly, it is patient-directed dying.

Euthanasia, in contrast to assisted or patient-directed dying, is when someone else administers to the dying patient a drug or lethal agent that causes death. In patient-directed dying, the patient self-administers the lethal agent; in euthanasia someone else does it.

"It's just the *idea* of suicide," Else said. "I understand the difference between persons who are dying and those who are not, but dying by your own hand has always been called suicide, and somehow suicide never seems right."

"Oh, wait," I said, breaking into her comment. "First, keep in mind, the word suicide is wrong—those who don't believe patients should control their dying use 'suicide' purposely to frame it as something bad or evil. And also remember that exceptions exist even to the prohibition against actual suicide."

"I suppose you mean like a soldier falling on a live grenade in order to save the lives of other soldiers standing nearby," Else said.

"Yes, that's an example. The circumstance allows it. In fact, we think a soldier is a hero for giving his life to save his comrades. His act is not suicide in the time-honored sense.

"Also," John said, "the Catholic Church teaches that some cases of ending your own life, for God's glory or for the salvation of souls, are not suicide.[8] Taking your life is not always suicide."

"Here's another example more like what John's thinking of doing," I said. "Remember the passengers who brought down

"Doc, I Don't Want to Die that Way"—The Story of John

the hijacked airliner in central Pennsylvania on 9/11? They prevented a different and even greater disaster by what they did. When they brought the plane down, they caused their own deaths and those of everyone on board. But because of the circumstances, we don't say they 'committed suicide.' In fact, we say they were honorable and valiant by giving their lives the way they did. These exceptions are rare but they show the importance of making a distinction based on the circumstance or condition under which a person takes his own life."

"Ah, yes, but that's different—those people were going to die soon anyway," Else said.

"That's just the point," John said, flaring up with renewed energy. "It's not different. The people on that airliner knew they were going to die. They didn't want to die any more than I want to die now. But they knew it was going to happen—soon—so they took things into their own hands and died their way rather than the hijackers' way. And they helped others by doing it. I'm like the people on the airliner—I'm going to die soon whatever I do, so I want to do it now, and save me and everyone else a lot of grief."

"Yes, I see," Else said. "But it bothers me that it might look as though you didn't try, that you took the easy way out, or just surrendered."

"Look," John said, craning his neck a bit more forward, "if I hadn't had surgery, which sure wasn't the easy way out, I'd have been dead long ago. Right? And I'd also probably be dead by now if I hadn't had the chemotherapy. Was that the easy way out—puking my guts out for weeks on end? So I've already put off dying twice. Far from surrendering, I was 'trying' when I went through those two treatments. I've done everything possible to stay alive, and it hasn't been easy. Now all I can do is wait and die slowly. What's wrong with dying now? How can that be suicide when I've *extended*, not *shortened*, my life?"

"Oh John, I'm sorry," Else said. "I know you didn't cop out. You went through a lot to stay alive with all that difficult treatment, and I know you did it for me, not yourself. You're right—you didn't surrender. It was the opposite of surrendering—and if you die your way, it won't be suicide."

After the three of us talked some more about how John's condition as a dying person is different from a suicide's, John's eyes drooped and I knew he was becoming fatigued. "I really have to get going or my wife will wonder why I'm so late," I said. But I had one more question: "May I ask about your religious or spiritual backgrounds? Knowing about that will help me understand your views on this matter."

"John and I were both born and raised Catholic," Else said, "and while we don't go to Mass regularly, we still believe in the basic teachings of our religion." She paused. "But we have trouble with some of the Church's edicts," she went on. "And we don't think God wants us to live on machines for as long as we possibly can by any means when our lives can no longer serve His purpose."

"Yes," John added, "this business of keeping people on machines as long as possible, even if they're unconscious and can't recover...hey, that's going too far. I can't believe God would want it."

"What about afterlife?" I asked. "Do you believe in an afterlife?"

"Oh, I don't know," John said. "Maybe, maybe not."

"I believe in an afterlife," Else said. "But I'm not sure what it'll be like."

"Well, then, here's a question for you: If you were dying, would ending your life—patient-directed dying—jeopardize your chance for redemption, or a good afterlife?"

Else had the look of the kid in class who never has the right answer. "That's what bothers me some," she said. "I don't think so, but how do you know?"

"No. It wouldn't!" John said. "I don't know whether there's an afterlife, but if there is one, God would want me to have a good one."

"Well, maybe." Else said. "I know lots of good Christians who feel the same way as you do about it."

Religious beliefs contribute greatly to an individual's attitude toward patient-directed dying, and people of faith hold disparate views on the issue. How they stand on the issue depends primarily on their beliefs about the afterlife. For example, taking a lethal dose of medicine would be unacceptable to dying patients who view death as the sole prerogative of God, or those who believe that hastening death under any circumstances would forgo redemption or bring damnation in an afterlife. On the other hand, many other religious people who believe in an afterlife consider patient-directed dying to be compatible with their faiths and religious beliefs.

While practicing Catholics, fundamentalist Christians, and Orthodox Jews are more opposed to aid in dying than others, in Oregon, 56 percent of Catholics and 60 percent of Protestants supported the law allowing it.[9] Many people of faith do not believe that God's gift of life means that one must live for as long as possible; in fact, some believe it is idolatrous to call artificially extended life sacred, or sanctified, when it only extends suffering.[10]

"Well, we've talked about a lot," I said as I picked up my coat from the chair where I'd dropped it. "But we have a lot more talking to do. How about if I come back again in a few days?"

"As soon as you can, Doctor," John said.

"Yes," added Else, "when can you come again?"

We made a date for six days later.

"Dr. Z," I shouted, when I saw him about to disappear down a hospital corridor. He waited while I caught up to him.

"Hi, Tom. Say, have you seen my patient?"

"Yes. Do you have time for me to tell you about it?"

"Uh, I'm very busy," he said, and hesitated, "but all right, if we make it quick."

We ducked into the doctors' lounge, and took seats away from the gaggle of other doctors.

"I had a good visit with John and his wife," I started. "They're both such nice people." I then told Dr. Z the gist of my discussion with John and Else.

"Doc, I Don't Want to Die that Way"—The Story of John

"Well," Dr. Z said, "I know what John wants, but my job is to help him live, not help him die. So even if it were legal for me to give him a stash of pills to end it all, I wouldn't do it. Patients can do what they want, but physicians shouldn't help anyone who wants to die. It's not our business."

"Of course," I answered. "Physicians shouldn't help just anyone to die. But what about someone like John—shouldn't it be legal for physicians to prescribe medicines to help him and other terminally ill patients die, if they choose to do so?"

"We shouldn't let just any doc do it," Dr. Z said. "You or I could do it carefully, but there are a lot of docs out there who aren't so careful, or who might be talked into it. People would die who don't really want to die, or don't need to."

"How would docs be talked into it"? I asked. "How would it happen?"

"Well, the family might convince the patient it was time to die—to save on expenses, or to protect the family coffers, or to collect life insurance. The family might convince the doctor that the best thing for the patient is to die."

"You've got to be kidding," I blurted out. "Dr. Z, stop a minute. You're not thinking this through. Physicians would have to be drawn in as unwitting accomplices. Could a patient who didn't want to die and was 'talked into it' by a relative convince a physician to write the necessary prescription? Or, would a physician write a prescription for a patient when asked for it by the patient's friend or relative? And if somehow the pills were obtained, what would make the patient take them if he didn't want to die? The most potent protection there could be against the sort of abuse you're

Patient-Directed Dying

worried about is the requirement that the patient himself must ask for and take the lethal medicine. Do you really think a patient would do that unwillingly?"

"Doesn't matter. I'll bet it would happen," Dr. Z said.

"Think about it. Suppose a patient who doesn't want to die does talk a physician into a prescription, takes the pills and dies. Sooner or later others in the family find out what happened and start an investigation. The physician gets found out, probably loses his license, and has a court case on his hands. It only takes one suspicious family member to ruin this physician's life."

"Or suppose a family member is the one who requests and obtains the pills and convinces the patient to take them against his real wishes. Someone else—a nurse, or another family member—will find out, and it's the end of that physician's career. C'mon, Dr. Z, you're not even willing to do it when the patient wants it and all the family members agree. Why do you think another physician could get duped into doing it when his patient really doesn't want to die? There's nothing to gain for docs in doing it—there's no money in it. And you know how paranoid docs are about legal or disciplinary action. Even the most careless physicians know they have everything to lose by providing pills for someone who doesn't want to die. Getting duped in this way is almost impossible."

"But how about poor patients, or those with no insurance?" Dr. Z asked. "Won't some of them ask their physicians to help them die?"

"Doc, I Don't Want to Die that Way"—The Story of John

"Unlikely, if not impossible," I said. "As you know, in our country patients with no means of paying end up in emergency rooms or hospitalized under Medicaid or as nonpaying patients. Would you write a prescription for someone you never saw before he or she was admitted to the hospital? Poor patients are the ones who are least able to have the sort of ongoing doctor-patient relationship necessary to accomplish what they want, especially aid in dying. Patients who don't have access to the health care system, and aren't able to obtain adequate medical care, are totally absent from reports of aid in dying in this country. In Oregon, all patients who have obtained a prescription for lethal medicines under the law have had ability to pay for medical services, including adequate end-of-life palliative care."[11]

"But if aid in dying were legal," Dr. Z said, "wouldn't docs be pressured or given incentives from insurance companies and HMOs to use it? Wouldn't these health plans want physicians to enable early dying as a 'quick fix,' allegedly 'putting an end to the patient's suffering' while also ending the need for costly end-of-life care?"

"Again, Dr. Z, I urge you to think it through. How would you react if an insurance company or HMO tried to influence you, very subtly, to arrange to have patients end their lives? Would you detect any such influence? Of course you would. You and every other doc involved would blow a whistle so fast and so loud the insurance company or HMO would be exposed almost immediately. And what do you think would happen to the price of the stock of a privately held HMO or managed-care corporation that was exposed as encouraging physicians to enable their patients to die for cost-cutting purposes"?[12]

"Maybe," Dr. Z said, "but I wouldn't put it past government-run agencies like Medicare or Medicaid, or the state-employee health insurance plans, to somehow get physicians to help people die early to ease the pressure on the budget."

"Dr. Z, that's not right," I said. "Physicians *always* resist someone else telling them how to practice. Do you really think an agency could influence or recruit physicians who would be willing to help them do that? Even docs who favor aid in dying for their terminally ill patients would detect and not tolerate any such attempt. Imagine the effect on the public, not to mention patients, if a single person in Medicare or Medicaid even suggested encouraging patients to die as a policy. It would be the instant undoing of any organization trying to do it, and you'd be leading the charge to disband the guilty agency."

"Look at it this way," I went on. "If a medical institution or a physician wanted to profit from the early deaths of patients, the obvious way to do it would be with patients who are on chronic life-sustaining therapy. Compare the 'cost savings' potential for a patient attached to a ventilator in an intensive care unit versus a patient dying at home, with or without hospice care. To pull the plug on the first patient would result in far greater cost reduction than providing pills to the second patient. That's obvious, isn't it, Dr. Z? But have you ever seen it happen? Have you ever even suspected colleagues of hastening death by withdrawing life-sustaining treatment against the wish of the patient or her family? Of course you haven't, because there's no gain for the physician in doing it, and a big-time loss for getting caught doing it. For all the same reasons, abuse of patients because of financial incentives to physicians for encouraging them to die early is highly unlikely."

"You know how it works, Dr. Z:

"Doctors do things that make them money.

"Doctors absolutely avoid things that don't make them money and can get them into trouble."

"Maybe you're right," Dr. Z said, "but I just don't want to be involved."

* * * *

Six days later I saw John as scheduled, but by then things had worsened for him. His lung cancer was causing him increased shortness of breath, and he had coughing fits when he couldn't clear the secretions from his throat. He told me he thought he "was running out of gas," and that he had made an appointment to see Dr. Z the next day. "I'm going to ask him again for the pills," John said. "Do you have any advice on how to ask without putting him off?"

"Not really," I answered. "At this point you just have to be straightforward. Tell him you appreciate all he's done for you, and the extra life he's given you, and ask if he'll help you go peacefully, your way. Tell him you're not sure you'll ever take the pills, but want them as security."

It was an ordeal for John to get from home to Dr. Z's office, but Else had driven him there many, many times before. This time he was determined to confront Dr. Z. After he and Else sat a half hour in the exam room, Dr. Z came bustling in, looking cheerful as usual, with his nurse behind him.

"Well, John, how's it going?"

"Not very good. I'm having more trouble breathing, and I get those headaches."

"Look, John, we can make that better," Dr. Z said. "I've been looking at your x-rays, and your lesions are well situated for radiation therapy. Our radiation therapists are great with problems like this, and in a month or two they can shrink the tumors that are causing your problems. What do you say?"

John looked at Dr. Z and said nothing. Then Else said, "Dr. Z, John doesn't want any more treatment. He wants to go—he wants to end it. I don't want to lose him, but we both think it's time."

"But you don't understand," Dr. Z said. "If the treatment works, and it usually does, he could have another good six months. Maybe more."

John looked back at him and said, "Dr. Z, if you want to help me, please give me some sleeping pills—enough to do the job. Doctor, please help me die."

"That I can't do. You're nowhere near needing that. Trust me, I know what you're thinking, but if the treatment doesn't work, we can take care of you. We'll take care of any problems that come up."

John looked at Dr. Z and slowly shook his head. He said nothing more.

"We think now is the time for hospice," Else said.

Dr. Z's expression went blank, but after a few seconds he said, "Okay, we'll help. Talk to my nurse." Dr. Z reached down, lifted John's hand, and shook it. "Let me know if I can help with anything." And he left the room.

John and Else never saw Dr. Z again.

After John signed up with hospice, his breathing continued to worsen and he needed an oxygen mask most of the time. On consecutive weekends his son Bill from Atlanta and his sister who lived an hour's drive away, visited him. John appreciated the visits, but both the son and the sister avoided deep conversations, and neither broached the subject of John's impending death.

I next visited John about a week after he saw Dr. Z and had joined hospice. Else was there, as she was most of the time, and now she slept every night on a cot she had set up in his room. After we had chatted for several minutes, John looked at me and said, almost sheepishly, "Doc, I'm sorry I messed up."

"What do you mean?" I said. "How did you mess up?"

"Oh, you know," he said. "I didn't do it right. I waited too long. I should have started earlier, as soon as I knew the diagnosis. I should have gotten pills from Mexico or somewhere, and saved everybody all this trouble."

"John," I said meekly, "I'm not sure there's a 'right' way to do it. You haven't had it too bad until now, and I know you're really upset to be in this condition, but you're getting good care and you're still at home, where you want to be. Else and I won't let it get too tough for you."

Patient-Directed Dying

John took a few breaths in and out as fully as he could, and then said, "Doc, don't blame Dr. Z for not giving me the pills. He couldn't help it."

"Yes, it's just the way he and a lot of doctors are," Else said. "But do you think they'll ever change? Do you think people in this country will someday believe it's all right to let dying patients end their misery? What are they going to do a generation from now when half the population is lying around wanting to die because they're old and incapacitated and miserable?"

"I know what you mean," I said. "Attitudes will change, but probably slowly. No one knows when the idea that patients should be able to direct their own dying processes will become acceptable enough to help people like you."

"Doc, just keep working on it. Okay?"

"Okay."

I was lucky to have seen John then, because just two days later he had a large stroke, after which he was nearly unconscious as far as the hospice nurses could determine. He groaned or grunted occasionally, but he didn't move on his own. It wasn't clear whether he could sense pain, so the nurses gave him enough morphine to be sure he had no discomfort, and gave him fluids through his intravenous line.

His son Bill and his sister Kathleen caught flights the day after the stroke and "camped out" in John and Else's house, while his sister Susan drove over every day to be with her father and mother as much as she could. To the dismay of all of them, Else, Bill, Susan, and Kathleen, they could not communicate with John. The hospice nurse, after consultation with the hospice medical doctor, said that most likely John had bled into his brain. It was clear he would never regain consciousness.

I was out of town the day of John's stroke, but returned two days later and heard Else's plaintive report on the telephone message machine. I hurried over and found a house suffused with despair and silent anger. We went into the room where John lay, connected to the world by a dripping intravenous line. It was to be his final treatment, the end of a dying process that conformed to orthodox medical practice.

We all stood by the bed, speechless and motionless. During times like this, when the situation is worse than hopeless, the competent physician should offer some scrap of solace or gratitude, spoken with the lavish assurance of his profession. But for a boundless time I had nothing worthy of saying.

Then Bill, the son, spoke to his father: "Dad, Dad, we love you," he said softly. And then, with voice rising, he said, "Why in God's name have they let this happen to you?" And then, looking straight at me, "I know you're not his doctor, but couldn't you have stopped this from happening? Couldn't you have talked to Dr. Z and made him help my father die without having to go through all this?" And then, shouting over his mother's stricken voice, "Where the hell is Dr. Z? Has he ever been here? Has he even called to see how Dad's doing?"

"Now, now, Bill, control yourself, it won't do any good to curse Dr. Z," Else said.

"What has medicine come to," Bill continued, "when a doctor abandons his patient at the end? Is it just big treatments and scans they think about? Don't they know there are people inside these bodies? Why isn't he here, with us, now?"

"Yes, now I realize John was right," Else said. "This is what he was trying to avoid when he asked Dr. Z for those pills."

"I wish Dad could have done that," Bill added, softening his tone. "If our society were compassionate it would allow dying patients to end their lives rather than forcing them to suffer as long as possible."

"Maybe we're the ones who have to change if the doctors won't," Else said.

"You're probably right," Bill said. "If I had paid more attention to Dad we might have avoided this."

"I think we're all realizing that Dad didn't get his final wish, and we're blaming ourselves," Kathleen said. "I think we should go out to the other room."

And we did.

Half an hour later the hospice nurse arrived. After she had checked on medicines and fluids, and had done a brief physical examination on John, I had a chance to talk to her. "Why is he still getting his routine medicines, and intravenous fluids?" I asked.

"Oh, we wouldn't ordinarily do that," the nurse replied, "but when I suggested to Mrs. H that we would stop all treatments if she allowed us to do so, she said not to stop them because she 'didn't want to be the person who made him die.'"

"Oh my," I said. "Let me talk to her."

"Doc, I Don't Want to Die that Way"—The Story of John

With the nurse still in the room with John, I sat down with Else, Bill, Susan, and Kathleen, and we discussed the situation. I said the obvious—keeping medicines and fluids going would only prolong the agony—and assured Else that she would not be the cause of John's death. In these modern times, I noted, the way we die means that someone, the patient or one of the patient's loved ones, has to make a decision about when to die. With support from her son and two sisters, Else agreed, and then told the nurse to stop everything.

Overnight John developed pneumonia. After consultation with the family the hospice nurse did not treat him with antibiotics. The nurse increased the morphine dose, and John died 24 hours later. His family was with him at the end, but unfortunately, he had not been able to tell them how much he loved them before he died. And, Else, Bill, Susan, and Kathleen didn't have the chance to tell John how much they loved him. They will always regret it.[13]

John didn't die his way.

CHAPTER 3

DYING MY WAY—THE STORY OF MARCIA

Marcia M. was a friend of a friend, and I met her when she was nearing the end of her life. She was as feisty as they come. Her appearance and personality were equally wiry, and at the hospital where she was a nurse she ran a "tight ship" on her medical floor. The doctors loved her, but they knew not to get in her way. She wasn't about to let other people tell her what to do—she'd make her own decisions, thank you.

And Marcia was now at a crucial decision point. Two years before, she had been diagnosed with one of the more aggressive and severe types of leukemia. She was then age 48, and until she became ill she was as active as a politician's caddy, and in between working long shifts at the hospital she especially liked skiing in the wintertime and hiking in summers. But over the brief time of a week or two she became tired just taking short walks, and felt totally fatigued halfway through a normal workday.

When Marcia had first learned and digested her diagnosis, she was devastated. "Marcia seemed stunned," her primary care doctor told me. "That's not unusual, of course, when a patient first hears the bad news, but she just sat there shaking her head, mumbling 'It can't be; it can't be.' And then, after I had spent about 15 minutes talking about chemotherapy and her great chance for a remission, she asked me for sleeping pills—'enough so I won't wake up.'"

"She was clearly depressed," he concluded. "She needed antidepressants, not a lot of sleeping pills."

Perhaps her doctor could have done a better job of breaking the news, but as most of us who have done it know, there is no "good" or nice way to tell a patient she has what is probably a fatal disease. Maybe he thought that Marcia, being a nurse who knows the ins and outs of this disease from having cared for patients with it, would want nothing but straight talk. Maybe if he'd been more empathetic and had talked with her longer she wouldn't have reacted so strongly. But simply to prescribe antidepressant pills was to shirk his duty; even an informed medical professional like Marcia needs comforting and the presence of human understanding and sympathy at such a time.

True enough, too many doctors react to all their patients' emotional problems by routinely handing out pills. But it's also true that some physicians don't recognize, or simply ignore, the emotional distress patients experience when learning bad news. At least Marcia's doctor was aware of her emotional response, and he was addressing the problem in his way.

Marcia's response was not uncommon. Patients sometimes even experience increased physical symptoms because of the emotional shock of a fatal diagnosis. Understandably, some patients' first thought is that dying would be the best escape from impending suffering. This reaction—termed a "panic response" by some, and "reaction formation" by psychologists—is frequently a cry for help. As Marcia later told me: "I went ballistic when I got the news, it was so sudden, and dreadful. Maybe as a nurse I knew too much. I couldn't make myself think it would all turn out okay."

News of the sort Marcia got is too much to process quickly—most patients require months, maybe years to adjust emotionally to the potential drastic change in their lives. No patient should consider hastening her death until first seeing if medical therapy is effective, either by curing her or adding good-quality time, or by providing good palliative care. Only then, without the coercive distress of pain or other physical discomfort, should she think through her options of what to do. In most cases, addressing the immediate problem of the patient who screams, "Kill me and take me out of my misery," will allay the anguish that breeds a panic response. Marcia had successful medical treatment for her panic reaction—antidepressant pills and counseling—and was then able to confront her condition calmly.

"It was good to settle down, and not go off half-cocked," she told me. "I think the tranquilizer helped. It allowed me to make the most of things, and I'm grateful for the remission I've had. And it gave me time to think things through. Now, when it's getting rough again, I'm not at all happy about the outlook, but I'm all right. I have things pretty well worked out as to what I want to do."

At first Marcia was skeptical about chemotherapy, based on her knowledge and her experience in caring for patients with her particular disease. But after she got over the initial shock of having leukemia, she opted for aggressive chemotherapy and went through two months of "living hell," as she later called it. She had a good remission, lasting 10 months after the chemotherapy was over, but then her symptoms returned and soon she needed blood transfusions almost every week. A second course of chemotherapy was just as tough on her, and although she had another remission it was shorter than the first one. "This is the way it usually happens," she told me. "It was worth doing to see if I could have a longer remission, but now I've come to the end of the road."

Her doctors, though, were recommending even more aggressive treatment: a bone marrow transplant. It works well for some patients, but for others it's—well, in Marcia's words, "worse than living hell."

"I've seen it all before," she said, "in patients dying with all sorts of different diseases. Chemotherapy and other treatments are worthwhile—very worthwhile—up to a point. But once you get going on the medical track, it's almost impossible to stop. They plan it all for you, where you go, what you do, and in the end they even program how you will die. Well, I don't want all that stuff patients go through at the end, getting every new treatment the doctors can think of."

Dying is now medically managed for most people. This what Marcia meant, although few people understand it as she does. A broad range of public-health measures has changed the course of our lives, from the beginning to the end. We live to "old age" because our waste goes to landfills and sewage treatment plants, our water is purified, and we get vaccinations. Instead of dying early in life from cholera, plague, or smallpox, we die decades later of heart disease, stroke, and cancer. It's a huge change from how people died just a couple of centuries ago.

Medical treatment also alters how we die. People are cured every day in doctors' offices and hospitals, with antibiotics, surgeries, radiation therapy and by other means. And most patients who have incurable diseases receive medical care that prolongs their lives for days to years, until new complications or conditions of treatment overwhelm them later in life. Most of us now die of new conditions created by medical technology and physicians.

"Without getting treated with chemotherapy, blood transfusions and antibiotics, I would have died from infection or bleeding early in the course of my leukemia," Marcia said. "That's the good part of medical management," she added—"getting more good time beyond when I would have died without treatment."

Chemotherapy didn't cure Marcia, but it postponed her death for almost two years. Now, the proposed last-ditch effort, a bone-marrow transplant with only a small chance of a long-term cure, would most likely just postpone her dying. Bone marrow transplants work well for some patients, but Marcia talked to medical friends and knew her odds were against another good remission. And, if she survived the transplant she would still probably then die slowly, and possibly from a complication of the bone marrow transplant itself. It's like a medieval walled city under siege with no chance of outside help: you can surrender and hope for good terms, or try to hold out but with the likelihood of slow, total decimation.

The practitioners of modern medicine sanctioned by society have changed how most of us die. After our Faustian bargain with modern technology lets us live longer, the price we pay is prolonged dying, often with increased suffering. This medical prolongation of the dying process is probably the single greatest driver of patients' desire for patient-controlled aid in dying. Most of us living today will face potential prolonged suffering at the end of our lives. In the years ahead, medical technologists will find still more ways to extend our dying processes, meaning that end-of-life suffering may become an even greater problem. We need to act now to change how we are allowed to die.

I was sitting in the living room of Marcia's small apartment. All around me, on the walls, on her desk, and on every end table, were photos of her while hiking or skiing in various wonderful-looking places. She also had books in unsteady piles on her desk, on the coffee table in front of the sofa, and on the floor in a corner. I looked at the titles: murder mysteries, a Bible, and some collections of poetry. Two poems she had written were on the wall, framed.

"Oh yes, I used to be into writing poetry," she said. "I never did get any of them published, but my friends say they're great, and I always liked trying to put my feelings about nature and the out-of-doors into words. Now I'm not writing any poems because I don't have the energy to do anything

Patient-Directed Dying

out-of-doors. I still love it, but it doesn't seem to love me anymore."

Marcia stood and walked slowly to the window, being careful to stay close to something she could hang on to if she lost her balance. She looked out the window to the lake in the distance and the mountains beyond. "Sometimes I think maybe I should have let nature take its course."

"What do you mean?" I asked.

"Oh, you know very well what I mean," she said with a mock frown. "Maybe I shouldn't have had all that chemo. It gave me more time, but now I'm caught up in medical dying. The doctors have mapped out how I'll die and I can't die naturally. I'm far past that."

Marcia had put her finger on another of the features of modern dying: very few of us die truly naturally. Man-made interventions result in medically managed—not natural—ways of dying.

In ancient times birth, living, and dying were all held to be under divine control; the fate of any individual was in the hands of the gods. Later the Hippocratic physicians introduced the concept of the *natural* cause of diseases. Maybe they incorrectly attributed diseases to an *"imbalance of the humors,"* or to diet, but by asserting that diseases had natural causes they broke with the old way, which attributed diseases to supernatural powers, or the will of the gods. With this new way of thinking about diseases people also began thinking that life and death also had natural, rather than supernatural, causes. This marked the beginning of an enduring conflict about how far mortals—physicians in particular—can go without violating what came to be called the "will of God."

Since this great shift at the time of Hippocrates, physicians have attempted to alter the natural courses of diseases, and by at least the 17th century they had acquired some means for extending life—amputations, or operations to drain infections, for example. In time, issues arose over the line between natural and unnatural. Philosophers and others questioned how man's intervention altered what we call nature. Can we really differentiate, they asked, between those of man's endeavors that are part of nature and those that are not? Don't a multitude of human actions amount to interference by man in the works of nature? Isn't it precisely the purpose of modern medicine to alter the natural course of disease in humans?

Today physicians prevent natural death by treating almost all forms of diseases and injury. If we were to restrict the modern practice of medicine to what is truly natural, we would return to a time before the Dark Ages. Modern medicine is an unfettered succession of unnatural (man-made) acts that render any principle of "natural order" unworkable. Physicians today "play God" and tinker with nature just as much when they cure people as when they help them die.

The consequence of medically managed living is artificially extended dying with medical management to the end. This is what Marcia was saying. And it is why she correctly saw that choosing to die by taking a lethal dose of pills was no more or less natural than other forms of medically managed dying. When patients are terminally ill and wish to avoid the ravages and suffering of medically extended life, she believed, they should be able to control how they die. Patient-controlled dying is the last in a series of medical interventions in the prolonged process of dying.

Marcia turned away from the window and sat down. "The problem is," she continued, "if I have the bone marrow transplant I'll lose control over things. Other people—doctors—will be making all the important decisions. They'll put me in the intensive care unit. Medical residents will be writing orders on me. The docs are the ones who'll decide whether or when to stop and how I'll die."

She looked at me a bit sheepishly and said, "Look, I really don't have anything against doctors, you know that. It's just that they have their own agendas with patients who are dying, and most of them want to keep going until their patients' bodies stiffen. Their agendas often aren't mine."

Marcia knew well how, unless someone dies suddenly, as from a heart attack or stroke, or by accident or violence, they'll be subject to an almost unending series of medical decisions and interventions, most of them made by physicians. Dying is a process, from the onset of the fatal illness to the moment of death, and any intervention during the process changes the ultimate time and form of death.

It's important to understand the central involvement of physicians in how we die today. The underlying terminal illness initiates the dying process, but physicians and their interventions change and steer the course of dying. Any and all decisions to extend life by treating an ultimately fatal illness are decisions to defer death to a later time, when the patient's condition will be different and dying may be more difficult.

"At the end, who should decide how I die?" Marcia asked. "Should I leave the matter to physicians? Will they direct my course of dying according to *my* values and directives, or theirs? You know how they make decisions," she said, looking at me. "Their decisions about how someone dies come straight from medical textbook algorithms for what to do for a given medical condition. 'Medicine by the book.'"

"Yes," I admitted. "A dying patient gets placed on an artificial ventilator because it's 'good medical practice' to do so, even if it just keeps the patient's body tissues alive while he or she can do nothing more than stare at the bright lights on the ceiling of the intensive care unit."

"I don't have to do it," Marcia continued. And then she looked at me and asked, "What do you think? Am I wrong to go against medical advice? Should I be a good girl and do what they say? My pastor is with me on this, by the way," she added. "He says I should do what I think is best for me."

"There's no right answer that fits everybody," I said. "Just tough choices. As you well know, a medical recommendation boils down to being told what to do if you want to pursue more medical therapy. Beyond that, sad to say, we doctors often don't consider anything else but the best medical treatment. So you have to look at it as the *medical* recommendation, as what to do if you choose the medical track. But if I hear you correctly, you're looking for the whole-person recommendation, the 'what's best for Marcia' recommendation. And for that, I agree—Marcia knows best."

"I was only ten years old when my grandmother died," Marcia said, "but I remember how it happened. She had a stroke, couldn't talk, and drooled a lot. My parents took her to the hospital, where the doctor ordered a feeding tube put through her nose and down into her stomach, and they kept her alive for three months. She had one infection after another, which they treated until she finally died because her heart gave out. My parents would come home after being with her at the hospital all day and say, 'She's suffering, she's suffering, but there's nothing we can do for her.'"

"What really bothered me was how my parents never once questioned what the doctors were doing to her. I always wondered about that. Why didn't they stop what was happening, and take her home to die peacefully? By keeping her in the hospital they were doing something—they were adding to her suffering, and that was wrong. In dying, doing nothing is doing something, and it can be the wrong thing."

"Watching how my grandmother was treated while she was dying, and how no one spoke up against what was happening, made me want to go into nursing to help older people avoid all the bad things that happened to her. And as a nurse, I've seen it all over again with so many patients. I often say, 'Doctor, why are you doing that, when you know it won't really make your patient better, and will only add more months of suffering before she dies?' Other nurses do the same, and sometimes the doctors listen to us, but mostly they don't. I don't think this way of treating dying patients will change until the patients and their families step in and say, 'No more treatments—just help her die without suffering.'"

Many people no longer hold the fatalistic belief that a dying person must accept whatever happens as being beyond his or her control. Over the last half century people have increasingly participated in the momentous medical decisions that direct their course of dying.

"You aren't a control freak just because you want to die in a manner consistent with your goals and beliefs," Marcia said. "Doctors think patients can't make important medical decisions, especially when the doctor disagrees with a patient's decision. Some docs even laugh at the idea of patient self-determination at the end of life, saying patients don't know enough about the different treatment options available and that they're influenced by their families."

"But that doesn't mean I can't make my own decisions based on the information I have," Marcia went on. "After all, doctors trust patients to make life-and-death medical decisions about things patients know nothing about—like the guy who's hurting like hell from a heart attack and they're asking him to give informed consent for coronary bypass surgery. Let me say this: a patient who has had an ultimately fatal illness for months or years is in a much better position to make a good decision about how to die than most patients are when they make major treatment decisions in hospitals every day."

"Yes," I said, "the important thing is for you to make the decision that best suits your goals. The way you die is based on human decisions, and you have every right to be the human in control of those decisions."

"I know," Marcia said, "that if I don't control how I die, someone else will. Why should I have to die the way somebody else says to do it? When I get to the end and it's a matter of someone deciding how I'll die, I want to be that someone. I'll do it my way."

*   *   *   *

After Marcia refused the bone marrow transplant she remained stable for about a week, but then began feeling weaker, and her blood counts worsened. She was losing ground. Her oncologist, Dr. F, pressed her to have the bone-marrow transplant. "You're only forty-eight," he reminded her sternly. "You need this. I know it's a long shot, but we've had a lot of good results with it, and it's your only chance to get well. If you don't do it, you won't last more than two months. You've got to do it."

Marcia's daughter, Nancy, was with her at the visit, and Dr. F looked at her: "You don't want to lose your mother, do you? If she doesn't do this, she'll go quickly."

Nancy was ambivalent. She knew her mother well, knew her aversion to treatments that only prolong the suffering of the dying. But she also didn't want to lose her mother. "Mom, can't you at least think about it?" she asked.

"I have thought about it," Marcia snapped. "I've thought about it for a long time, and I've made my decision. I won't give in. It's not how I want to die."

Dying My Way—The Story of Marcia

Marcia and Nancy soon left Dr. F's office and they never saw him again. Later that day Marcia phoned her primary care physician who agreed to enroll her in a home hospice plan.

Why do so many physicians like Dr. F insist on treating to the very end, when the treatment is likely to be of little benefit and often extends the patient's dying process with increased suffering? Why can't they let go of the professional goal of using every possible treatment, and concentrate instead on helping their patients die peacefully, especially when that's the course the patients want to take? To be sure, there are many physicians who do a good job at stepping back from curative treatments and helping their patients with palliative care at the end, but many more—specialists in particular—don't do a good job.

The reasons are complex, but center on two professional traditions, one modern, the other ancient.

Modern physicians are trained to cure diseases, and they do it successfully. But the very success of curative therapy distracts them from attending to their patients' other needs, such as comfort care at the inevitable end of life. This emphasis on "curing" rather than "caring" leads physicians to keep prescribing more treatment while often overstating the chances of recovery and minimizing the treatment's risks or unwelcome side effects. The medical training of physicians is to cure people, not to help them die. And in the culture of hospitals, curing is the supreme goal. This use of burdensome or painful procedures or treatments with low or remote chances of success often results in needless suffering by prolonging the process of dying. Physicians' zeal to heal often leads to increased suffering.

For every dying patient there comes the time when the physician realizes he has no more useful therapy, and he "gives up." Unfortunately, since many physicians think their purpose is solely to cure or to prolong life—to "heal," as many say—at the time of giving up they withdraw from their dying patients because they "have nothing more to do."

This withdrawal is an ancient practice. In the Hippocratic writings of more than two thousand years ago, physicians are cautioned to stop seeing patients when it becomes obvious that they are dying—probably to protect the physician's reputation, which would be tarnished by association with multiple deaths.[14] The tradition of withdrawing from dying patients still holds among many, like Dr. F, who disengage from their patients once curative treatment has ended.

Marcia had decided, based on her knowledge of the perils of end-of-life treatment, that she would want to end her life before she survived to the very end of a medically managed painful or debilitating illness. Ten years before her leukemia struck she had joined an activist right-to-die organization, and every year she updated her advance directives for medical care. She was divorced and out of touch with her former husband. Now her only child, Nancy, was ready to support her in whatever she decided.

In fact, just before starting her first round of chemotherapy, Marcia had made preparations for hastening her death when and if she thought it would be necessary. She had approached her family doctor, Dr. W, whom she had known for more than ten years and liked very much, and asked if he would help her get some "insurance," meaning pills. She assured him that she had no intention of using the pills then, and promised to go through with the chemotherapy, but said she would feel more secure "just to have everything in place." Dr. W, who knew her feelings about how she wanted—or didn't want—to die, listened to her, probing her reasons and giving her assurance that if things got really bad he would see to it that she got good comfort care.

Finally, he said, "I'll tell you what, Marcia. I'm not just trying to put you off, but I think it would be best for both of us if we wait awhile. We should give ourselves more time to think about this. We both need to be sure we're doing the right thing. How about making an appointment to see me again in two weeks. We'll talk about it then."

"Fair enough, Dr. W. See you in two weeks."

Two weeks later Marcia sat gowned and waiting in Dr. W's exam room, wondering what he would say. When he entered and sat down next to her, Dr. W said, "For the last week I've thought a lot about what you asked me. How do you feel about it now?"

"The same," Marcia said. "I'd really like the pills as a backup. I don't want to get caught in medical purgatory."

Dr. W knew it was illegal to prescribe pills for the purpose of his patient's ending her life, but he understood Marcia's condition and her desire, and felt deeply that it was his duty to help her. He also knew that merely having the pills would give Marcia the peace of mind and security she wanted, and, furthermore, she might never take them. He wasn't recommending that she take them to die, and that wasn't his intention, but he was willing to let her choose how to use the pills.

"All right," Dr. W said, "I'll write the prescription. But I want you to give the chemo your best shot."

"Thank you, doctor, thank you. And don't worry. I'll do it."

Now it was just a week after Marcia's first visit from the hospice nurse, who set a schedule for weekly visits but said she would come more often if necessary. Marcia could feel the disease beginning to overwhelm her. She was weaker by the day, and she knew that infections and fever and—most likely—bleeding under her skin and inside her body would happen next. She would soon be losing control of her body. The time to leave was near, and she set a date.

Marcia now did what she had had in mind for more than a year: she asked Nancy to try to find her former husband—Nancy's stepfather—and tell him what was happening and what her plans were. She also had previously told two close friends and her pastor, all of whom supported her. She had kept in touch with her right-to-die advocacy organization and had a close relationship with one of their volunteers, a woman close to Marcia's age. The volunteer was helpful in talking to Marcia about getting her affairs in order and preparing for the final event, and had by then become a trusted friend.

About noon on the day Marcia had chosen to die, Nancy came into Marcia's room and said, "I have someone who would like to see you."

Dying My Way—The Story of Marcia

Marcia's estranged husband Fred then walked into the room, looked at Marcia, and said, barely able to get it out, "I had to come when I heard what was happening. I had to see you before you leave us." He went to her and they embraced, their faces joined beneath tears, both mouths whispering "I'm sorry."

Fred sat down, Nancy left the room, and he and Marcia talked for about twenty minutes, hand in hand. Neither talked of the separation or of the bitterness of the past. They remembered the good times, and laughed and cried. When Marcia tired visibly, Fred said, "I know what you're planning to do. May I be here with you this evening?"

"Of course. You must."

That evening Nancy, Fred, two friends, the pastor, and the advocate volunteer gathered in Marcia's small apartment. Marcia was weak but in good spirits, and with Nancy's help she had colored her paleness with makeup. For almost an hour everyone sat talking, mostly telling stories about Marcia, some of them funny enough to make everyone laugh. Marcia talked about her life and how she cherished it and was sad to lose it, and mentioned her happiest moments and her disappointments and regrets. She spoke of her love for everyone present and how much she appreciated all they had done for her, and she asked them to forgive her for the times she was unpleasant or unappreciative. Of course they all said she had never been that way!

When Marcia said the time had come, each in turn hugged her and spoke again of their love for her, to which she responded in kind. Then the pastor said a short prayer and told Marcia she was a fine and loving person, beloved by her Lord.

Marcia had prepared a cocktail with the medicine in it. Now she picked it up, looked around, and said, "Hemlock, anyone?" She drank the cocktail swiftly, put the glass down, and pushed back in her chair as well as she could. "Odd, isn't it, that this is all going to end," she said. "Thank you all so much for being with me."

Amid expressions of solidarity, the visitors held her hands and hugged her again, each one of them teary-eyed and holding back their sobs. Marcia's face emanated fulfillment and harmony. Within five minutes her eyes drooped, and a minute later she was asleep. Nancy and Fred sobbed openly. In another twenty minutes Marcia was gone.

Marcia had found goodness and purpose in life, she was with her friends at the end, she had their love, they had hers, she was lucid and able to say good-bye, and she had spiritual peace. Hers was a dignified and peaceful death—it was the way Marcia wanted to die.

CHAPTER 4

WHEN IDEOLOGY TRUMPS COMPASSION—THE STORY OF MICHAEL

Michael C. prepared for dying. He was an 81-year-old retired carpenter and cabinetmaker with heart disease, and had contacted Compassion & Choices, an advocacy organization that works with and advises dying people. He had asked for information about dying peacefully, and as part of the organization's response, I went to see him. From information he'd been sent prior to my visit, he knew I would be prepared to discuss with him any and all questions he had about patient-controlled dying. He also knew that I would not be his physician and would not provide him with a prescription for a lethal dose of pills.

The first time I went to his house Michael was sitting up in a recliner in the living room with a blanket wrapped around him. I liked him immediately, maybe because of the way he took my hand in both of his without letting go and fixed his eyes on me. He knew I was a physician and a cardiologist, and I knew he had severe congestive heart failure—his heart was so weak he could do nothing more taxing than turn over in bed. But his heart was strong enough to keep his brain working well, which was evident within seconds of hearing him speak.

When Ideology Trumps Compassion—The Story of Michael

Modern medicines can keep patients with severely weakened hearts alive for years, sometimes decades, after they would have died without treatment. I have been fortunate to know the look of gratitude in the faces of hundreds of such patients. Michael had that same look of hope, confident of help. But it wasn't hope for improvement of his heart. During the last twelve years he had had every treatment possible for his weak heart, and by now he knew he was at the end of his cardiac rope. His hope, I learned quickly, was that I would help him get the means to die.

"Doc," he said, "I've always been an active person. I was always doing something or going somewhere. Now I don't even have the energy to hold a book on my lap and read. For three months now, all I can do is sit here—I even sleep here because I can't lie down without being short of breath. My feet and legs ache constantly with all that water in them," he said, slowly pulling the blanket up to expose his greatly swollen feet. "The swelling goes all the way up to my thighs, Doc."

"I can't do a thing by myself," he went on. "I can't walk, and even talking like this tires me out. All I can do is watch television." He pointed to a portable commode and added, "My wife even has to help me get on this thing. It's not right. Nobody should have to stay alive this way. What do you think, Doc, would you want to keep going if you were in my shoes?"

We talked privately for about half an hour, while I tried to understand who he was and why he wanted to die. Then Michael's wife, Judith, came into the room and joined the discussion. "She has reservations about what I want to do," Michael said.

Patient-Directed Dying

"It's just…well, I don't know why he's given up," Judith said. "His doctor says he's depressed, and I agree."

"Of course I'm depressed," Michael said, showing a bit of anger. "Why shouldn't I be? It's depressing to be dying."

Most dying patients are depressed to some degree because the awareness of dying and the effects of the disease itself are both depressing. As Dr. Elizabeth Kubler-Ross pointed out decades ago, most patients who die slowly go through an identifiable stage of depression.[15] Unlike the panic reaction some patients have when they first learn they have a fatal disease, this depression is situational—a normal reaction to the losses associated with dying. It is not the cause of the wish to die, but a symptom of knowing that life is ending.

"Doc, let's face it," Michael said. "I have no hope for recovery, or for even improving. I know it will just continue to get worse, as it has for the last year, and I can't do anything but watch and wait. Just a year ago I made a cabinet down in my shop, but now I couldn't even get downstairs. The one thing left I can hope for is an easy passage to the end."

"Hopelessness" is the psychological symptom most correlated with the desire to die, whether quickly from the fatal disease or by aid in dying. But because hopelessness and a "wish to die" have long been two of the major criteria for clinical depression, a dying patient like Michael, who says he has no hope for regaining meaningful life and therefore wishes to die, is commonly misdiagnosed as clinically depressed—that is, having an actual mental illness aside from the underlying terminal illness.

To feel hopeless is not an unexpected or irrational response to dying. What appears as depression in most dying patients is a natural expression of sadness and grief, a sense of loss of life and purpose, and can be a normal response to dying.[16] Michael's talking about having no hope was not a sign of mental illness.[17]

The use of medicines and counseling to treat the common situational depression of dying patients may help relieve their symptoms of grief and loss. But many dying patients resent being treated with antidepressants; they feel it is an unwelcome intrusion on their feelings—a chemical frontal lobotomy. And treating their depression seldom changes their attitude about wanting to die, nor does it affect their decision making.[18]

When Michael's hospice nurse suggested he take an antidepressant, Michael said he "didn't like pills messing with my head," but at his wife's urging he agreed to take the medicine. It seemed to make him more cheerful, but he remained steadfast in his desire to die.

Ongoing pain or severe physical symptoms are not the most common reasons dying patients make *sustained* requests for hastened dying. Most patients who carry through patient-directed dying have had good palliative care. All patients in Oregon who request a lethal dose of pills under Oregon's Death With Dignity Act (see Appendix 1) are screened to be sure they have first had adequate palliative care, and 89 percent receive hospice care.[19] This percentage is many times greater than the average for all dying Americans in all the other states (where aid in dying is not legal).[20] Patients choosing to hasten their dying want to control the time of their death to avoid the suffering—to whatever extent—of slow dying even with the best of palliative care. This is not a "cry for help," but a decision founded on their basic values and a desire to die at a time and by the means of their own choosing.

Michael's wanting to control the final stage of his dying was not a sign of clinical depression or curable mental illness—it was an act of affirmation, self-esteem, and dignity congruent with values developed over his lifetime.

* * * *

Fatigue, Michael's constant companion, worked on him. His eyes drooped intermittently and with effort he pulled himself back into the conversation I was having with Judith. "My wife wishes I'd act happier," he said, "but we've talked about what I want to do, and she'll help me when the time comes. I have a source," he said, glancing around to be sure no one else was present, "for getting the necessary pills to end this existence."

Judith looked down and nodded slowly. Neither of them ever told me from whom or how they thought they could get the pills.

"By the way," I asked, "what about the rest of your family? Those must be your children in the photos I saw hanging on the wall just inside the front door. Do they know what you want to do?"

They both spoke at once, but Michael stopped and Judith went on. "We have two daughters and a son. One daughter lives in Baltimore, so we don't see her a lot, but she was here

When Ideology Trumps Compassion—The Story of Michael

for a few days over last weekend. I think she knows what Michael wants to do, but she's never said what she thinks about it."

"She's all right with it," Michael said. "She told me she'd help me if that's what I want to do."

"Our son lives in Albuquerque, and our other daughter lives here in Seattle, about a 15-minute drive from here," Judith continued. "Michael hasn't talked to either of them about this."

"That's not quite right," Michael corrected her. "I've talked several times with Paul, our son, about how I feel about not going through this business to the bitter end, and he agrees with me. He has no problem with it. But that other daughter of ours, Jill, the one who lives nearby, she'll never like it."

"What does that mean, 'she'll never like it'?" I asked.

"It means she'll never agree to it. This is my problem. She's 'born again,' and she says she won't let me 'kill myself.' She'll try to keep me from doing it."

"And how about you?" I asked. "Would you want to do it against your daughter's will?"

"It would be hard to do. I can't do it if she's against it and won't let me," Michael said. "I'd lose her forever if I did."

"What do you mean, 'lose her forever'? If you die, won't you lose everyone forever?"

"Well, I won't exist after I die, but I don't want to lose her love before then. If I do it against her will, I'll have lost her love. Even more important, I don't want her to live the rest of her life angry with me, unable to feel my love for her. And if I do it without her permission, she'd always know she didn't give me her love, and someday she'd regret that mightily. I'd rather she feel my love forever. So if Jill doesn't allow me to do it, I won't. But for myself I don't see anything wrong with it."

The three of us were silent, and still.

It is not at all uncommon for someone close to a dying person to object to that loved one's plan for patient-directed dying. When a daughter, for example, first learns of a parent's terminal illness, her response is often similar to that of the patient: shock and denial. Above all, this close loved one feels the grief and agony of her own impending loss. As part of her reaction to the probability of losing her father, a daughter will do everything possible to keep him alive. She will smother him with attention and love. She might search the Internet for a possible cure or at least a treatment to slow the dying process. She will make sure her father takes his medicines, she will drive him to his medical appointments, and she will urge him to remain upbeat.

Above all, she will resist anything that might shorten his life—particularly a plan to die. This is a very natural reaction. It is saying, "I love you too much to let you die," and it's also saying, "I do not want to suffer the loss your dying would cause me." On one level the reaction is an expression of love for her father; on another level it's an expression of selfishness—by opposing her father's wish she protects herself from losing him.

The daughter needs time for grieving, for reconciliation with her father, and, as often happens, for becoming able to support his wishes. In time—weeks to months usually—a

When Ideology Trumps Compassion—The Story of Michael

daughter who *shares her father's basic values* will usually overcome her own sense of loss in order to honor her father's desire to die. She may not like losing him, but she will do it for him.

This does not ordinarily happen when the daughter (or any close loved one) holds a "principled" objection in conflict with the dying parent's beliefs. If the objection is based on a deeply held religious conviction—that terminating one's own life in any circumstance is "evil," for example, or that a doctor who writes a prescription for a lethal dose is "killing"—the daughter is unlikely to relent, and she may do everything possible to thwart her father's plan to direct his dying. In such cases the daughter may even report her father's plan to the hospice nurses or the attending physician. More than once I've known of a dying patient's child who threatened to go to the police if anyone aided the parent in dying.

It is therefore *essential* for a patient and those who support him to gain the approval or at least the acquiescence of *all* the close loved ones with whom he will be interacting at the end before undertaking to die by his own means. This means talking to loved ones soon after the diagnosis is known, in order to give them time to assimilate the news and work through their despair of impending loss. If a dying patient knows that a particular child or relative will oppose his wishes on grounds of religious principle, he may choose to exclude that person from knowledge of his plan to direct his own dying. But any loved one who is likely to be present in any capacity at or near the end should be included in the plans.

Patient-Directed Dying

A week later when I met with Michael and Judith, at their request their daughter Jill was present. She was an attractive woman, smartly dressed. I may have been imagining it, but when our eyes met I saw daggers coming at me. She was seated, and when we were introduced she said hello but declined to stand or shake my outstretched hand. I knew it would be a tough meeting.

After some awkward small talk, I turned toward Jill and said, "Your father and mother and I have been talking about your father's condition, and they want to include you in the discussion."

"Then you better know right away I won't have anything to do with your plans," she said. "He's my father and I'm going to take care of him."

"What's your understanding of your father's plans?"

"I'm not going to let you kill him," she bristled.

Neither Michael nor Judith said anything. I pointed out to Jill that her parents were honorable and ethical people, and it wasn't a matter of killing but rather her father's wish to halt his medically prolonged dying process.

"He doesn't have to do it. I'll take care of him," she repeated without looking at me.

We talked some more, but as is typical of such encounters, the ideological distance was too great to bridge. When I left, Jill stayed seated.

Later in the day I phoned Michael and Judith and advised them to defer making any plans for hastening death (patient-directing dying) until or unless Jill relented in her firm opposition, which I thought would be unlikely.

When Ideology Trumps Compassion—The Story of Michael

"We've come to the same conclusion," Judith said. "We're both really afraid of what might happen if Michael got the pills and went through with taking them. There's just no telling what Jill would say or do if that happened. It could be awful."

"Yes, we better not try it," Michael said, having joined the phone conversation on another line. "But it does rankle me. I always try to compromise, but people who hold absolutist views about morality never compromise, and it seems I'm always the one who gives in, which is what I'm doing with Jill. Wouldn't that bother you?"

"Oh my, yes," I said. "I know what you mean. Absolutism always smothers tolerance and compromise. You see it happen frequently, in business, in politics—everywhere. But Michael, you don't have the luxury of enough time to stand firm and work for a compromise. And of course—and I hesitate to put it this way—Jill will be around for a long time after you're gone, and I know you are willing to give up what you want for her happiness, even though you don't share her views on the matter."

"That's it," Michael said. "Two wrongs don't make a right."

In circumstances like Michael's, where a loved one knows of a patient's plan or desire to end his life, and adamantly opposes it, it is best to abandon the plan. The discord and anger that could persist among the surviving family members for the rest of their lives makes going through with it not worthwhile, despite the patient's desire for it. Jill's anger at her father, and at her mother, brother and sister who supported her father, could have rent asunder the family, perhaps forever. Michael knew this when we had talked about Jill a week before, I now realized. Giving in to another's values on such an important issue is not being weak willed, but rather an acting out of deep love that, even if unreciprocated, is probably worthwhile to prevent a lifetime of ill will among the survivors. Someday, perhaps, being honest and treating our adversaries with respect may help them to do the same for us.

"Why does Jill call it killing?" Michael asked me rhetorically. He was still slumped back into the recliner, but he held his head forward and his eyes were alert. "Of course I'm against killing. Isn't everyone, except maybe a few criminals? But if I'm already dying, why should ending my life before it's absolutely necessary be called 'killing'? No one's killing me. The disease is killing me. Why should a doctor compassionate enough to write a prescription for me be called a criminal when he's already kept me alive longer than I would have lived without his treatments? Why do so many people think this way?"

"Here's my take on it," I offered. "No doubt about it, some people think that aid in dying is 'killing.' But it isn't. The definition of 'kill' is 'to deprive of life,' and to deprive is 'to take something away from.'[21] Like the word suicide, the word 'killing' misrepresents what's happening for two reasons. First, no one takes something away from the dying patient who retains full control of whether to take the prescribed dose. Second, the terminally ill patient who dies by voluntarily taking a prescribed medicine is not deprived—on the contrary, he achieves his goal. He ends his life, but he doesn't deprive himself of something he wants. Patient-directed aid in dying is not killing, nor is it a wrongful act.

"But isn't it a matter of God's law forbidding it?" Judith asked. "We're Christians, but I don't know what to think about this. Wouldn't Michael's ending his life violate God's will?"

Now I knew I was in for a longer visit. I excused myself to call home and say I'd be late for supper, came back to the living room where Judith was now seated next to Michael, sat down, took off my sweater, and the three of us settled into a long discussion.

Although the majority of Americans think dying patients should be able to end their lives in order to end suffering, the notion that patient-directed dying violates divine law, or "the sanctity of life," has deep roots in our culture.

Primitive human beings were helpless against the forces of nature. They had no control over birth, illness, the threats to life all around them, or death. They attributed these events to the supernatural, as the workings of the fates or the gods, and submitted to the will of the gods in all matters relating to life and death. For the most part, physicians of ancient and medieval times worked harmoniously with religious laws and teachings; they were viewed as agents of the gods, or of God. But when human healers acquired the means to modify the courses of various illnesses, they raised the enduring question: What is the appropriate role of healers with regard to how mortals die? Does man transgress the realm of the divine, or of God, by preventing death, or by helping someone die? In modern parlance, should doctors "play God"?

Patient-Directed Dying

Judeo-Christian teachings say that every human is formed in the image of God, and it is God who gives life, and therefore life is sanctified, or made holy. The early Christian church viewed abortion, euthanasia, and suicide as violations of the sanctity of human life, and thus as sins against God's work, and physicians were enjoined from aiding in these practices.[22] The dominance of the sanctity-of-life principle has survived to this day in our society, whether one views it as a religious or a social concept. For those who hold this view, to violate the sanctity-of-life principle is to kill, which is a sin or crime.

"But," said Michael, "why would God want us to sanctify suffering? Why should it be against God's will to end a life that has already been extended far beyond its natural limit?"

"I have to agree with Michael," Judith said. "Once doctors keep someone from dying naturally, they're already playing God. And if they can keep someone from dying naturally, they ought to be able to help that person die later on, when the extended life they have produced becomes too brutal to bear."

"I think it's all a question of God's purpose," she continued. "Does God want us to sanctify all life, however much we change it for better or worse, or only life as He made it? If it is God's will that we may intervene and alter people's bodies and lives, wouldn't God let us end life that we have made unendurable?"

Judith had gone to the heart of the issue: exactly what life should we sanctify? The sanctity-of-life principle developed during the Middle Ages, at a time when physicians were not

When Ideology Trumps Compassion—The Story of Michael

dealing with patients whose lives had been unnaturally altered by surgery, chemotherapy, or organ transplants.

In the 13th century Saint Thomas Aquinas equated the realm of God's law with "natural law," or everything that is natural, including all human life.[23] Thus, under "natural law," any attempt to help a patient die—under any circumstances—violates natural life, or the sanctity of life. To this day, church teaching stresses the sanctity of all natural human life. For example, *in vitro fertilization* is a violation of God's law because it is not a natural means of conception. Whether you approve or disapprove of *in vitro fertilization*, there should be no argument—the procedure is not natural.

When we equate "God's law" with "natural law" in talking about dying patients, we run into a problem: what do we call "natural?" Church leaders speak of sanctifying life "to the time of natural death."[24] But, if the principle of the sanctity of life compels us to sanctify natural life, must we sanctify life when it is no longer natural? Although today very few of us die naturally, by common practice we seldom even think of how unnaturally our lives are extended. Most people say, for example, that a cancer patient who has had life extended by chemotherapy and surgery, or a patient who has had thirty years of insulin treatment, dies "naturally" when complications of treatment finally lead to death. We even say a patient with an artificial heart dies naturally if and when the heart is turned off. The scope of what is natural, and therefore by church teaching must be sanctified, has expanded over the centuries by calling all new forms of human life "natural."

Unfortunately, defining "natural" human life has become part of the larger "culture war" in the United States. In the Terri Schiavo case, for example, many "pro-life" adherents argued that removing Terri's feeding tube was an act of "killing," even though she was in a persistent vegetative state. Along with denying that she was in a persistent vegetative state—contrary to medical findings—they argued that she was not at the end of her natural life. This is an important cultural-religious point, because to agree that any patient being kept alive with a feeding tube is being kept alive artificially—not naturally—would be to give ground by using secular, medical criteria rather than religious criteria to define the limits of natural life.

It is important, therefore, for those who advocate the sanctity of *all* human life, to maintain the extension of life by medical technology as an extension of natural life, which is therefore subject to "natural law" and to the principle of the sanctity-of-life. Accordingly, on March 20, 2004, Pope John Paul II said that to remove the feeding tube from any patient in a persistent vegetative state would be "…*a serious violation of the law of God, since it is the deliberate and morally unacceptable killing of a human person.*" He further stated: *"I should like particularly to underline how the administration of water and food, even when provided by artificial means, always represents a natural means of preserving life, not a medical act."* [25]

The pope framed artificial as natural. This makes allowing someone to die by withdrawing a feeding tube an act of killing, even if the patient has indicated through an advance

When Ideology Trumps Compassion—The Story of Michael

directive a wish to die if she is unconscious and has no chance for recovery.

"But it doesn't make sense," Judith said. "By this way of thinking, when doctors prolong someone's life through artificial means, it's "natural" and they're carrying out God's will, but if the same doctor later helps that same person die he's violating the sanctity of life—he's killing.

"That's right," I said. "The church says we must sanctify life 'to its natural end,' but then says almost all life is natural, no matter what artificial means doctors use to prolong it."

"I agree, we should sanctify life to its natural end," Michael said. "But when is that? Why should we sanctify life when it has been extended beyond its natural end and a person is suffering and there're no medical techniques to cause him to recover? I don't think that's God's purpose. I think it's disrespectful for someone to say my life is sanctified when I think it no longer is, according to my beliefs."

Should we hold sacred all forms and conditions of life, no matter how much they have been distorted by medical technology? Are we beholden to sanctify all future forms of life engineered by cell or DNA therapy? Must we sanctify unnatural life we have prolonged and made painful and undignified? To do so would be a failure to adapt to modern methods of how we die, and would be bound to wreak great harm on future dying patients.

Our society must face its responsibility for what it has done—it must acknowledge its intervention in changing the forms of human life, and should allow a parallel human intervention to help humans die without unnecessary suffering. We need to sustain our moral codes and laws that prevent killing, but legalize aid in dying as a humane response to life that has been extended medically beyond the bounds of nature.[26]

* * * *

I saw Michael about once a week, and for almost a month he seemed better. He hadn't changed physically for the better, as he was no less short of breath, and his feet that peeped out from beneath the blanket he kept wrapped around himself seemed barely able to contain the swelling. But he seemed less aggravated with life, or his condition. "I'm resigned to it," he said, when I commented on his more placid demeanor. "Virtually all the time I'm awake I'm so tired I just wish I could go to sleep and not wake up. But I'm not going to fight with Jill about it. I'll manage…somehow. But don't stop visiting me Doc, I may need you," he had said at my last visit.

Early the next week the phone rang. "Michael says it's time," Judith said.

"Time for what?"

"Time to die. That's what he's saying."

"How's he wanting to do it?"

"That's what he wants to talk to you about."

"I'll come and talk to him," I said, "but surely he and you know I can't give him a prescription, and given Jill's attitude, there's no way he should consider ending his life with pills."

When Ideology Trumps Compassion—The Story of Michael

"He knows that," Judith said, "but he says you have another idea—some other way of letting him go faster."

"All right. I'll be right over."

When I walked into the living room Michael was in his recliner chair, as always when I visited, and he looked as if he'd somehow fused seamlessly with it. At first glance I detected no change, but small changes aren't obvious when you see someone too often.

I found the change in the lack of bounce in his voice. Before, Michael's voice had seemed soft and weak, in keeping with his faltering heart, but his words had had a lilt to them, which now they had lost. It seemed he couldn't interrupt the little air he was pushing out of his lungs for the luxury of talk.

"I'm ready…to go," he said, almost whispering.

"Let's get you sitting up farther," Judith said, knowing intuitively to get the level of Michael's heart up above the backflow from the pools of blood in his distended legs.

"Is it getting tough now?" I asked.

"Yes," Michael said less haltingly. "You once told me….I could die peacefully…by stopping eating."

"Yes, you can do that, if you're ready. But we have to talk about it."

While Judith took notes, I explained how, during the final stage of their diseases, many patients lose their appetites and stop eating up to a week or more before they die. This phenomenon is especially prevalent in patients with cancer, and

Patient-Directed Dying

is due to decreasing function of one or more organs. Almost all of us have known someone who couldn't be coaxed into eating, or even drinking, for days before dying of a prolonged fatal illness.

If, before coming to this last stage of not wanting food, a terminally ill patient voluntarily stops eating and drinking, he will die in a matter of days, usually 3–12 days, depending on how well nourished he is prior to stopping food and fluids, and how successful he is at resisting food or fluids. Death comes from dehydration, and anybody—even many dying patients—can live weeks without food if they have water or fluids.

Patients usually experience thirst and hunger for the first two or three days after voluntarily stopping eating and drinking, but in most cases these symptoms can be suppressed or alleviated with moist swabs or ice chips applied to the inside of the patient's mouth. Morphine is very effective in suppressing symptoms. After a couple of days with no food or water, bodily changes suppress a person's appetite, but it's still best to swab the mouth regularly and give enough morphine to keep the patient comfortable and unaware of physical symptoms. A patient who receives sufficient attention and adequate treatment will die peacefully by this technique. And once it's clear that the patient is not eating or drinking, medical personnel are usually willing to give enough morphine to provide an even more peaceful passage to the end.[27]

After I had explained to Michael and Judith how this works, Judith asked, "Michael, is this what you want to do? You really haven't been eating much for the last week, anyway. Maybe you won't miss food so much. Do you think you can do it?"

"Yes, I know I can do it," he said, "so long as the hospice nurses don't object, and will give me what I need so I won't feel hungry."

"Your hospice nurses will want to know why you want to do it," I said, "but if you're honest with them and say it's what you want to do and are determined to do, most nurses will work with you. You have to bring them on board, so when they realize you're not eating they won't try to make you swallow liquid nutrients, or give you sugar-water through a needle."

"How about if I eat this evening, but nothing more starting tomorrow?" Michael asked, looking at Judith.

"If that's what you want, that's what we'll do," she said.

I had to add, "Don't forget, you can always change your mind. It's your decision. But stopping food and liquids, then allowing yourself a little something to eat or drink, then stopping again, back and forth, never works. That only makes things worse."

"It's all or nothing," Michael said.

"Should I tell the children?" Judith asked me. "What about Jill?"

"Yes, tell them, tell them all. Jill will see soon enough that Michael's not eating, and she needs to know what's happening and that her father will soon be gone. And your other children who don't live nearby need to know so they can get here to be with their father at the end."

"Yes, I'll phone them right away."

Patient-Directed Dying

I assured Michael and Judith I would be back the next day, and soon left them to themselves and to their thoughts, which I could scarcely imagine. I knew I was emotionally involved, but I also knew I had to keep my ship on an even keel, for them. It wouldn't be easy.

When I visited Michael the next evening I found him in his usual place. Jill was crouched on the floor beside him; she seemed concerned and solicitous, but not agitated or angry. Michael responded to my greeting, but kept dozing off after a sentence or two. The combination of insufficient oxygen and morphine had the effect, I thought, of a late-afternoon lecture in medical school.

"He had some morphine thirty minutes ago," Judith said. "It's odd, but his breathing actually seems better."

"Not medically odd," I said. "Morphine is a great drug for severe breathing problems if the dosage is managed by a professional. How did you get the morphine?"

"The hospice nurse came this morning and, as you said she would, asked him some questions. But then she told me how to administer the morphine, and how to take care of other things, like his eliminations. She was so good to us."

"She's a sweetheart," Michael said, arousing marginally from his morphine stupor.

"And the swabs she gave us work really well," Jill added. "I'll see to it that we keep his mouth from drying out too much. I won't let my Dad feel bad."

"Michael," I said loudly, trying to break through the morphine effect, "are you having any thirst?"

"Oh,…no…not much…it's all right."

"It'll be better tomorrow," I said. Michael dozed off again.

Their other two children, a son and another daughter, would be flying in tomorrow, Judith said.

After staying another 20 minutes and talking some more with Judith and Jill, I got up to go home, saying I'd keep in touch. Jill stood and said good-bye.

"We'd like it if you could stop in again tomorrow," Judith said as I was leaving.

The next day I was busy until late afternoon, so I phoned Judith to see how it was going.

"He's about the same," Judith said. "He hasn't asked for anything to eat or drink, but it's probably because he's sleeping a lot. The nurse said to give him morphine regularly, every four hours, without waiting for him to ask for it, and that's what I've been doing. He sleeps most of the time, but he opens his eyes when I shout at him."

"How does he look? Are his lips bluer than they have been? Is his breathing the same?"

"He looks the same," Judith said. "His lips are the same—they've been a little dusky for weeks now. And his breathing…well, every now and then he seems to stop breathing for maybe 10–15 seconds. When I first noticed that I got worried, but the nurse says it's common in people who are on morphine."

"Yes," I said, "and it also happens to patients who are getting close to the end. But remember, the most important thing is whether he's comfortable."

"Yes, he is," Judith said. "And by the way, our son and our other daughter arrived last night, and it's a big help to me to have them here. Michael recognizes them, and I'm sure he's very comforted to see them."

"Excellent," I said. "Sounds like things are going as well as can be expected."

We chatted some more and agreed I needn't make the 30-minute drive to their home that evening.

I saw Michael each of the next three days, and delighted in meeting his son Paul, from Albuquerque, and his other daughter Mary, from Baltimore. Michael responded when spoken to—or shouted at—but otherwise dozed most of the time. His breathing was as Judith had described it, with occasional pauses of up to 30 seconds without a breath—pauses common in someone dying of congestive heart failure.

But his appearance was unchanged. His skin did not look dehydrated, and I commented that usually people who get no water lose their normal skin turgor.[28]

"Are you giving him anything to eat or drink?" I asked.

"No, nothing," Judith said. "We're turning him regularly, and swabbing his mouth; that's all."

Then she asked, "How long do you think it will be until he dies?" It was a question she'd asked me on each of the five days since he'd begun his fasting. "Paul and Mary have to go home tomorrow," she added.

"It's unpredictable. I just don't know. I wish I could tell you, but it could be tomorrow, or a week from now. I really don't understand why things aren't going more quickly." And then I asked, "How much urine is he putting out?"

Michael had a catheter in his bladder, and Judith and the nurses had been measuring how much urine his kidneys produced every day. For the previous 24 hours he had made 400 ml of urine, almost as much as the first day after he'd stopped eating and drinking. This was less than a normal person makes in a day, but a lot more than one would expect from someone who hadn't had anything to eat or drink for five days.

"I don't understand this," I said. "He should not be making this much urine."

"He had an awful lot of water in him, with all that swelling from his heart failure," Jill said. "That's probably where it's coming from."

I knew that wasn't right, but didn't say anything. I had taken Michael's pulse and checked his feet and lower legs for edema—swelling—every time I saw him, and I knew his swelling was the same. It bothered me that Michael's dying was taking so long. He was not suffering, but it's always hard for family members to have to wait and watch, and Judith, Paul, and Mary wore clear signs of fatigue and emotional distress.

When I left, Judith followed me out onto the porch. "Who gives Michael his morphine at night?" I asked. "Who stays with him during the night?"

"Jill has stayed with him all night, ever since he stopped eating. It's been a godsend for me—it's the first time I've been able to sleep through the night in months."

"I hesitate to say this," I said, "but something's wrong. When a body gets no water, it holds on to all the water it has, and makes as little urine as possible. By now he should have almost no urine output for 24 hours. I just wonder if someone's giving him water."

"Maybe Jill's doing it," Judith said. "I'll bet she is. I can't believe it. I'll have to find out."

"Yes, if she or someone else is giving him anything to eat or drink, it isn't helping him, it's only prolonging the process of dying, which will make it all the harder on everyone."

"I'll see what I can find out."

Judith met me at the door when I arrived the next day.

"Ahhh," she said, betraying a reluctance to say what was on her mind. "When I asked Jill if she'd been giving Michael water, she just said, 'Why are you asking me that? Don't you trust me?' She never really answered the question. So I kept a close eye on things for the rest of the day, and I slept in Michael's room last night. I told Jill I wanted to be there. And guess what? Michael's urine output was only 70 ml for the 24 hours ending this morning."

"Well, look," I said, "it's pretty clear what's been happening. He's been getting water or juice or something, which is why he isn't changing. But don't confront Jill about this. She's undoubtedly doing it out of her love for her father—it's hard to look at someone dying without trying to help them, especially if you don't like what's happening. But now that Jill knows you're suspicious she'll probably stop doing it. Let's hope she can accept that her father has to die, and that his dying is peaceful."

When Ideology Trumps Compassion—The Story of Michael

"I won't ask Jill about it again," Judith said, "but I'll keep sleeping in Michael's room."

"Have you told Paul and Mary about this?"

"No. They both left today. They'll call when they get home."

"I wouldn't tell them. Just let it be."

"That's what I was going to do. They don't have to know."

By two days later Michael had changed. His lips were bluer, and his breaths were shallower and less frequent. His urine output was down to nil. Judith and Jill had said their goodbyes the day before, the last time he responded to them. It was now eight days since he had stopped eating.

The following day when I answered the phone I heard Judith say, "Michael died this morning. I was with him and he went quietly."

While the interventions of a multitude of doctors and their medical technologies gave Michael many extra years of good life, each intervention changed when and how he would ultimately die. Michael's self-determined intervention of stopping eating and drinking had also changed his course to the end, consistent with his goals and hopes. But his wasn't the last intervention—it was Jill's.

She had the last say by keeping him alive days longer than he otherwise would have lived. It wasn't Michael or Judith's way. And it meant that Paul and Mary weren't with their father at the end.

Chapter 5

WHO DECIDES?—THE STORY OF AGNES

One evening my wife relayed a request for me to see a dying patient, Agnes C. Agnes was a dear friend of a woman in my wife's exercise class, and during one of their power walks the woman poured out her concern for Agnes. Apparently Agnes, age 64 and dying of breast cancer, was now spiraling downhill with her disease and was talking about dying. Upon hearing this, my wife said, "She should talk to my husband."

"Of course, I'll be glad to talk to Agnes," I told my wife. "But be sure she knows I'll not be her doctor and I won't be involved in helping her die."

"No, no, nothing like that," my wife said. "She just needs someone who will listen to her and help her sort through all the medical issues she's now facing. You know very well how doctors never spend enough time talking to patients. Well, that's what I want you to do—talk to her."

And so it happened.

Agnes was born and raised in a small town about twenty miles from where she now lived in Seattle. Four years ago she was still the office manager at a downtown real estate escrow

Who Decides?—The Story of Agnes

firm. Her husband Henry was still practicing law, representing small businesses.

Henry met me at the door the evening of my first visit. He was a large man, and I reckoned he was about the same age as Agnes, or maybe a couple years older. Agnes' and Henry's daughter Stella, looking to be in her late thirties, soon appeared and joined us.

Henry led me to Agnes' room in their condo. It was an all-too-familiar scene: in the middle of the room a hospital bed with electrical controls for raising or lowering different sections of the bed; at one side of the head of the bed one of those long trays with a vertical arm for controllable height, with many "get well" cards standing on the tray; at the other side of the head of the bed a more conventional bedside stand, loaded with bottles of juices, medicine containers, and a wash basin. A horizontal bar was bracketed in place above the bed, positioned for Agnes to grab when moving. On the pole at the foot of the bed, and plastered all over the wall beyond that, were family photos of her daughter, son, and several grandchildren, as well as multiple crayon drawings with captions such as "get well, Grandma," and "I love you, Grandma."

In the bed, with a sheet and thin blanket pulled up to her neck, Agnes lay on her back, head propped up and eyes tilted to see me as I walked into the room. It was the picture I hoped not to see; it signaled more information than any hospital discharge note or summary. One need not be a physician to recognize the look of death—the sallow, waxy skin tightly drawn over the now-prominent cheekbones, the eyes retracted into their orbits as though afraid to see out, the head lowering slowly from its upward stare. To those less familiar with this picture it must be frightening, giving them urgency to find any means to restore the color, pull the eyes back out, and to see the loved one smiling happily. But to the experienced physician it is the picture of no return—the scene of a body ravished beyond restoration even by the miracles of our newest technology. After entering Agnes' room I hoped my facial expression wouldn't reflect the picture my mind was seeing.

"Hello, I'm so glad to meet you," I said, realizing that although I might possibly help comfort Agnes, most of the talking I was there to do would be with Henry and Stella, and, later, their son Benjamin.

"Hello, doctor," Agnes said, drawing out both syllables of the two words she spoke. "Are you my doctor? Or are you a friend?"

"Maybe a little bit of both," I said, "but mostly I'm a friend. I want to help take care of you and to make sure you're comfortable." After a few more introductory exchanges, I slipped into my comfortable professional role: "Are you having any pain?"

"Oh yes, I have pain most of the time. But the morphine helps it."

By then I could see that Agnes was having some trouble breathing. "How's your wind?" I asked.

"Not so good. But it's been this way for a while. I don't think it's getting worse."

We chatted for a few minutes more, and I was relieved to see that Agnes was clearheaded and seemed to have a reasonable idea of her condition. "You don't have a long time to get to know me," she had said at one point in our discussion.

When Stella suggested that her mother might be tired, Agnes looked at me and said, "Please come back and visit again."

"I will, of course."

Henry, Stella, and I went to the living room where they filled me in on some of the details of Agnes's illness. She had been diagnosed with breast cancer eight years ago. Her employer had been generous about giving her time off work during her surgery, chemotherapy treatments, and other problems that developed following the onset of her illness. But six months ago she'd had to stop work entirely because of problems arising from the cancer's recurrence—fatigue and pain that required medicines to control it. Two months before, when Agnes was hospitalized because of shortness of breath, tests showed fluid around one lung, which meant the tumor had spread to the lining of the lung. A physician drained most of the fluid—as much as possible—and that eased her breathing and made her feel much better.

Before leaving the hospital Agnes arranged to join a home-hospice plan, and had been at home since then. At first the hospice nurse came only weekly, but now she came two or three times a week because Agnes was having a lot of pain. The nurses treated the pain with a skin patch that contained a morphine-like drug, and Agnes could supplement with a morphine pill under her tongue if the patch didn't control the pain. She still seemed to enjoy food, but according to Henry she was eating less than usual and had lost about twenty-five pounds during the last six months.

A professional caregiver, Robb, stayed with Agnes five days a week, and also did housework. Henry worked at his law firm, but cut back his workload to be home four full days a week. Stella lived in Yakima, a 2½-hour drive from Seattle, and had taken a long weekend to be with her mother. She worked as a researcher, studying means of delivering better medical care to the children of migrant farm workers.

They both seemed eager to talk. "I don't want to see Agnes suffer," Henry said. I don't want to lose her, but I hate to see her this way. She's in bed most of the time, you know. She hasn't been out for a ride for at least a week now, and being up for more than fifteen minutes tires her out. And she's having constant pain—not severe, she says, but it's there most of the time. I think she's getting near the end. Isn't there something we can do?"

"What would you like to do, if you could, other than to cure her of her disease, which is impossible?"

"Well, I'm no doctor, of course, but I have enough doctor friends to know that doctors have their ways of sometimes helping their patients die rather than lingering to the very end."

"We want you to understand, Doctor, we're not asking you for anything," Stella inserted. "Mother already asked her doctor for pills to take when she is ready to die, but her doctor wouldn't have anything to do with that. He just brushed her off. She's not happy to have no control over what's ahead for her."

"But what's the difference," Stella asked, "between taking pills to die or being in a hospital and dying when the doctor gives you enough painkillers to let you die, or stops the machines that are keeping you alive? I don't see why one is any better or worse than the other."

"Exactly. Don't lots of doctors help their patients die, one way or another?" Henry added.

"Well, yes. We can talk about it," I said. Fortunately, I had lots of time, and didn't mind staying a while longer.

"The difference between aid in dying and what most doctors feel comfortable doing openly is mostly, if not entirely, in appearance. Most physicians do help some of their patients die by using various medical procedures, but they don't like to be seen as helping someone die. Why these procedures are acceptable, while for a physician to write a prescription for a lethal dose of pills is prohibited, is largely a matter of image, or semantics—how we verbally frame what physicians do. The key to whether a physician will help a patient die is whether the physician *appears* to be directly involved in the death."

"How, then, do they do it? Does it have to be something secretive?" Henry asked.

"No. The key is doing it in a way that appears to be good or accepted medical practice. Let me give you an example. When dying patients are suffering, physicians often give generous doses of morphine—often called a "morphine drip" when given intravenously—large enough to eliminate all pain or suffering. Sometimes, in order to be sure there is no suffering, they "snow the patient under" until death occurs. This is deemed legal and ethical, and is called the "double effect" because the first effect—intended—is to relieve suffering, while the second effect—not intended—is to cause death. It's extending or exaggerating an accepted medical practice. But, it's clearly medically managed dying.

"I've heard of this," Stella said. "Why isn't it called euthanasia?"

"Well …" and I took a big breath. By now I needed to get home. "How about if we continue tomorrow morning?"

"Yes, let's call it a day," Henry said. "I'm exhausted. But you better not forget where this discussion left off."

"Don't worry," I said. "See you tomorrow."

Driving home, I marveled at all the questions they had asked, and of their determination to keep discussing what must have been a difficult subject for both of them. It was as if they were having a conversation they had always wanted, but were never allowed to have.

When I went to see Agnes the next day, she looked more tired, and when she smiled weakly and thanked me for coming she spoke more slowly than she did the day before.

"Agnes didn't sleep very well last night," Stella said. "Pain. But I called her doctor and today we're giving her a double dose of some of her medicines. And the hospice nurse will be here this afternoon. You'll be better soon, Mom."

Agnes soon started to fall asleep, so Stella, Henry and I left her with Robb, the caretaker, hoping she could sleep, and resumed our talk of the evening before.

"So," Henry said, "why isn't giving a lot of morphine until the patient dies called euthanasia?"

"Because it's not purposely given all at once and in a large enough dose to cause death. But even if it does, it's not euthanasia, for two reasons."

"Everyone agrees that good and ethical medical care includes giving enough morphine or other drugs to keep a patient comfortable.[29] These drugs can and do cause sedation, but if a patient is already dying, it's not at all clear that even high doses of morphine hasten death. If a doctor doesn't use more morphine than is necessary to control pain, even if that dose seems very high, it probably doesn't hasten death. And when doctors give large doses of morphine to dying patients, their intent is not to end their lives, but to relieve suffering."

"Ah, yes," said Henry, peering out through his lawyer eyes, "but can't doctors hide behind 'intent'? It's often terribly difficult in the law to know someone's precise intent. Couldn't the good doctor give a dose he knew would stop the patient's breathing? How many docs take the time to determine the lowest dose that will take care of a patient's pain, and might not that dose change? And, do doctors themselves know their real intent when they pour in the morphine?"

"This is the problem. Doctors are certainly capable of having divided intentions—both to relieve pain and to shorten the time to death. I'd never want to guess at the intentions of most doctors who are treating dying patients, but I strongly believe that in almost all cases their intention is primarily to relieve suffering, even if the treatment hastens death. Doctors rarely know whether they've hastened a patient's death, but you're right—in truth I suspect they often don't mind if they do, if their patient is suffering."

Patient-Directed Dying

"But the point is," Henry continued, "if because of the treatment the patient dies sooner than he otherwise would, the doctor *is* shortening life—he *is* controlling dying. The doctor is the cause of the death. But no one screams that it's murder, or violates God's will. I don't think it's any different from giving a large dose of pills all at once."

"In terms of outcome, or what happens, it's not different," I said. "And doctors use another treatment that controls dying more surely and directly than a morphine drip or writing a prescription for a lethal amount of pills. In a procedure called 'palliative sedation,'[30] the physician gives the patient a sedative continuously (by vein or under the skin) to induce unconsciousness for the purpose of abolishing all sensation of pain. At the same time, all fluids, nourishment, and essential medicines are stopped, so the patient dies in a relatively short time, usually in two to six days. This procedure also is deemed ethical and legal."

"As I asked before, what's the difference between this and taking sleeping pills all at once and dying quickly rather than slowly?" Henry said. "Is it just a matter of timing, or the speed of dying?"

"Yes, that's it. In fact," I said, "some people even call this 'slow euthanasia.'[31] If a physician administers a large, lethal amount of a drug quickly within a minute or two and the patient dies soon after the injection, anyone would call it euthanasia because the injection immediately preceded death—it caused it. In contrast, if a physician uses approximately the same total amount of the drug but administers it in a much lower concentration and much more slowly, it causes only sedation, and death doesn't ensue until the patient dies days later of dehydration. Then, when the patient dies, there's no direct link with the drug—there's no smoking gun and people say the patient 'died naturally.' I know of a patient who died under continuous palliative sedation while his physician was on the golf course. No one with the patient at the time he died would have thought of the doctor on the golf course as having just assisted the patient in dying. But he did exactly that. It took a while, but the doctor's treatment caused the patient to die when he did—earlier than would have happened otherwise.

"How on earth," Stella wondered aloud, "can someone say that patient-directed dying by taking pills violates the sanctity of life while this procedure, palliative sedation, doesn't?"

"Again, it's a matter of semantics. We say the doctor sedates the patient to take away the pain or suffering, and since the patient has a legal right to refuse any treatment, the patient's decision to stop food and fluids leads to death. But you're right—the doctor is directly and intimately involved in helping his patient die—no less so than when he prescribes pills that a patient takes herself."

"Everything gets wrapped up in a neatly framed package, legally and ethically, doesn't it?" Henry said.

"There's one historical matter that bothers me," Stella said. "It's the Nazi experience with euthanasia. We're Jewish, and although we think that aid in dying is all right when done individually and privately, we worry about a law putting power into the hands of a state agency. In Nazi Germany it started with doctors doing Hitler's dirty work. If it became legal in America for doctors to help people die—even restricting it to those who are terminally ill—could it get out of hand, like the way the Nazis used euthanasia to eliminate people they didn't like, or didn't want? Aren't we brushing a little close to that possibility?"

"The Nazis practiced murder, not euthanasia," I said. "Furthermore, the 'right to die' movement in America is not asking for euthanasia. We're asking for aid in dying, controlled and done by the patient, not by a physician or anyone else."

During the early decades of the 20th century, movements in Europe and America gained some limited acceptance for a goal of improving the genetic stock of the population by sterilizing severely retarded or genetically defective persons. While the eugenics movement was dying out elsewhere in the world, the Nazis promoted the concept as a means of developing a "master race." They began with a series of laws or acts under the catchphrase of "social eugenics," by which they sterilized adults who were mentally retarded or had serious genetic defects.

Next they eliminated (murdered) children Hitler decreed to be severely mentally retarded or to have congenital or genetic defects, deformities or paralysis.[32] The Nazis called these crimes "euthanasia," hoping to gain cover for their murders as giving good deaths to people whom they labeled as defective and whom they said would suffer throughout their lives. It was a deliberate corruption of the word, intended to gain legitimacy for their killings.

Who Decides?—The Story of Agnes

The Nazis then began mass murders of Jews, Gypsies, homosexuals, and others whom they considered to be subhuman, without even invoking euthanasia as a cover for their killings. However, in the public press, and especially in the public mind, the Nazi mass murders continued to be called "euthanasia." As a consequence, ever since World War II the Nazi legacy has made people associate euthanasia with murder—particularly of ethnic groups.[33,34]

"So you don't think an ethnic group could be targeted in this country in the guise of aid in dying with help from physicians? Some people think it could," Stella said.

"To suggest it could happen," I said, "is an affront to our democratic institutions, our legal system, and to the people of this nation. It would require governmental policy or sanctioning."

"But German intellectuals and Jews said that Hitler would never get away with his madness, yet he succeeded in manipulating the broader public and some intellectuals who compromised themselves with the excuse that by joining the Nazi party they were more able to save people. Couldn't the same thing happen here, perhaps through a campaign in the public media?" Stella said.

"Stella, think, for a second or two, what this would entail," I said. "How would it happen? We now have great national debates over the death penalty for convicted murderers. We protest against police 'profiling' of minorities. We debate about whether suspected terrorists can be kept in jail or have the right to trial in this country. As a nation we would have to abandon all pretenses to civil rights. It would require a policy worse than slavery. To have physicians or others end patients' lives on an other than voluntary basis in this country would be impossible without the most cataclysmic moral and social change in our history. We must guard against abuses, but saying legalized aid in dying would lead to widespread abuse of ethnic or disabled groups is an irrational hypothesis.

Over the next two weeks Agnes's health deteriorated as she became weaker and more easily short of breath. Stella visited each weekend, and once drove over the Cascade Mountains during midweek to spend the night with her mother, driving back to work early the next morning. The hospice nurses visited two or three times a week and told Agnes to use the oxygen mask all the time, but she disliked it and kept pulling it off. Her pain was controlled for the most part with increased doses of morphine, and she began sleeping more.

I had visited Agnes about every third day, perhaps too often to notice small or subtle changes, but it was obvious to all of us that her breathing was more labored. I discussed this with Stella and Henry, and said it could mean a re-accumulation of fluid around her lung. I asked them to mention this to the nurse when she next visited.

From comments Henry made, I knew he had talked to two or three doctors he knew, hoping to get a prescription for the lethal pills Agnes wanted, but had had no success. And, by now, all the morphine Agnes was getting meant she was not capable of making good medical decisions, and so was past the point where she would be a candidate for aid in dying, as under the criteria in Oregon. Their hope for a quick and peaceful end had faded away.

On one of my visits I sat down in the living room with Henry and Stella, and our talk soon returned to how doctors can help patients die.

Henry mentioned a friend of theirs, a woman who had terrible emphysema from decades of smoking, and had lived the last month of her life connected to an artificial respirator in a hospital.

"That's what Mother would never want," Stella said.

Henry agreed. "Agnes visited this friend many times in the hospital, and thought it was barbaric to keep her connected to the respirator when there was no chance of recovery. 'Henry, don't you ever let them do that to me,'" she told me.

"Above all, Mom doesn't want to be hooked to machines in a hospital," Stella said. "She wants to die here, at home."

And then, out of the blue, Henry looked at me and asked, "Doc, have you ever stopped a breathing machine on a patient?" When I said "yes," he asked, "What happens when you do that? Does the person die suddenly, or slowly?"

"When patients need a mechanical respirator to stay alive, it means they can't breathe well enough on their own to stay alive for long. If they're disconnected from the machine, their body tries to make them breathe. Sometimes the patient's own breathing is effective enough to keep them alive for hours, but death usually comes after several minutes of gasping. If the patient is conscious and could be aware of suffocating, doctors give them enough morphine or other drugs to take away the sensation or distress of suffocating."

"So," I continued, "by withdrawing life-sustaining treatments like artificial respirators physicians directly end patients' lives. Another example is when someone cannot eat or drink and is being kept alive by a feeding tube inserted into his or her stomach. If a physician stops all feedings by withdrawing the feeding tube, his involvement in causing the patient's death is as direct as when he disconnects a patient from a ventilator—it just takes longer after stopping feedings. In either case, the physician's act leads to the patient's death. These procedures are legal and ethically correct if terminally ill patients wish it.

"When you disconnected your patient from a breathing machine, how did you feel?" Stella asked.

"It was very difficult," I answered, "even though we sedated him and he wasn't conscious when it happened. But what I did directly ended my patient's life—I knew it—and that wasn't a good feeling. But you know what? It was the best thing to do. His wife and children all agreed with his request that I do it, and it saved him and his family days or weeks more of his being tied to a machine in an intensive care unit until he died. After all, we put him on that breathing machine," I said, "and we had an obligation to take him off it when we saw it wasn't helping him. Even so, it wasn't easy."

Henry shook his head. "Wouldn't you rather just write a prescription for pills and let the patient take them himself? If I were you, I'd rather do it that way."

"Oh, yes, it sounds easier, but it's not easy that way either," I said. "And, a lot of patients get too sick to swallow pills, and they have no good way to die. Patients on artificial respirators, or with feeding tubes, can't swallow, but you can help them die peacefully by stopping the treatment that's keeping them alive.

"Soooo," Stella said, "if Mother were connected to a breathing machine to keep her alive, would you or most doctors be willing to pull the plug if she asked for it?"

"Yes, I would. And most doctors will do it if their patient has no chance for recovery and requests it, but there are still some doctors who won't do it because they consider it 'killing.' It's the old business of appearance—the association of the patient's death with the doctor's act of stopping the breathing machine makes some physicians say it's killing. However, any patient in this country has a constitutional right to stop or withdraw any treatment, even if doing so will predictably cause his death."

"So if Agnes were on a ventilator right now," Henry said, "she'd have a constitutional right to die. That's the law."

Now Stella piped up. "I can see what you mean, but aside from legal matters, doesn't it seem better to just stop a treatment and let someone die naturally on her own rather than to give pills that directly cause her death?"

"Stella," Henry said, "as the doctor said the other evening and just now, it's a matter of appearance. If someone dies a week after you pull out their feeding tube, it may seem like you're just letting them die, but tell me, who put that tube in there in the first place? And who was feeding the patient for

Patient-Directed Dying

months or years before pulling the tube? All that treatment wasn't just letting the person die naturally. It was actively doing something that you later stopped. Same thing for pulling the plug on a respirator."

"So," Stella said, "what happens if the patient doesn't ask to stop the treatment—or can't ask? Does a patient on a respirator or a feeding tube just keep on living indefinitely until he dies of some other cause?"

"Yes," I said, "unless the patient has an advance directive asking for the treatment to stop. Once a patient who won't recover is on life-supporting treatment, someone must make a decision about what to do. And commonly it's the patient's family that must decide, because the patient is unconscious or unable to make decisions. Either way, keeping or stopping the treatment, requires a decision. If the family wants to keep going with the treatment, it requires ongoing decisions to maintain treatment until the patient dies of some other cause.

"But," I went on, "stopping treatment of some sort to allow someone to die—whether it be antibiotics or blood pressure medicine or a pacemaker—is very common. Half or more of the people who die in this country do so after a decision to stop treatment.[35] Ironically, the movement for patient self-determination means that making decisions about how we die has become a part of modern dying. In the old days, before life was so frequently prolonged, the one thing a dying patient didn't have to worry about was deciding how to die—the disease did it for her. But today the dying patient—or her family or friends—have to decide when to stop the treatment. And that's tough."

Who Decides?—The Story of Agnes

Henry cleared his throat, closed his eyes for a second to recharge his mind, and then continued. "If a family decides to let a loved one die by withdrawing a feeding tube, instead of making everyone agonize while the patient dies slowly from lack of water and food over days or more than a week, why not just administer a high dose of sleeping medicine through the feeding tube before taking it out? The result would be the same, but it would be ever so more humane and compassionate."

"Of course it would," I said. "The key decision, the one that must pass ethical muster, is not how you help a person die, but whether and when it is proper to help a patient to die. After the decision to stop treatment—which should be based on the patient's wishes as known from an advance directive such as a living will—the means of allowing the patient to die is secondary, in my opinion. But here's where appearance comes back into the picture. If a physician were to administer a lethal dose of medicine through a patient's feeding tube, it would look like killing. On the other hand, allowing the patient to wither away slowly from absence of water and food has the appearance of just 'letting her die.' But it's wrong to look only at who is doing what at the moment of a patient's death. This is a narrow view, and it neglects earlier decisions that prolonged the patient's life and forced a later decision about how she would die.

"All these other ways doctors have to help people die—morphine drips, continuous palliative sedation, withdrawing life-sustaining therapy—they're legal and ethical, aren't they?" Stella asked.

Patient-Directed Dying

"Yes, they're legal and ethical and they help a lot of patients die peacefully," I answered. "But remember—physicians are directly involved in using these procedures to assist in deaths that are not natural. We just need more general awareness that, for terminally ill patients who choose to do it, patient-directed aid in dying with pills is also a humane way for doctors to assist in deaths that are not natural."

"Oh, don't we ever," Stella said.

When I saw Agnes a few days later, she looked much the same, and Henry said she was eating about the same as before. I instinctively felt her pulse, which was rapid and not strong.

"I wish you'd visit more often," she said in a barely audible whisper.

"Why, are you tired of seeing Henry and Stella?" I joked.

"No, it's the conversations you have with them. They tell me everything you say. But I wish you'd do your conversing here, in my room. I can hear, you know."

I was embarrassed, and ashamed. For years I had preached to medical students about not standing outside patients' rooms where they know you're talking about them. And I also had always told them that patients who appear to be unconscious often hear and understand what we are saying about them at their bedsides.

"I'm sorry. From now on, we'll hold our discussions in here."

"All that business about stopping treatments to let people die is very interesting," Agnes said. "It makes me mad, though, that I don't have a way to die when I'm ready. I wish I lived in Oregon, or some place where I could get the pills to take. I'd do it now if I could; I'm just putting in time. I can't believe how fatigued I am. All I want to do is sleep."

Tragedy struck three days later. Before Henry went off to work that morning, he had talked with Agnes, who seemed the same, and then went over instructions for her care with Robb. At 1:45 that afternoon Henry's phone rang at work and a woman's voice said, "Mr. C., you better get to the hospital, quickly. Your wife stopped breathing, but the medics got her going again and brought her here, to the hospital." Henry could hear beeps in the background.

He was stunned: "What? But why? Why did they do that?"

"Because she stopped breathing."

"But she had a 'Do not Resuscitate' order!" he shouted. "And she's in hospice. She wasn't supposed to be taken to the hospital. She can't be there."

"Sir, when your wife stopped breathing the caregiver called the medics. I'm sorry, but the medics don't have time to call around and find out what the family wants them to do. Their policy, and ours, is to resuscitate if necessary, and then get the patient where he can be taken care of. I hope you understand."

Henry didn't understand, and his distress quickly turned to fury. Agnes had a living will that included a DNR [Do not Resuscitate] order, saying that in case her heart stopped or she stopped breathing they should let her die. She had a copy of this on the refrigerator at home as well as at the foot of the bed where she slept at night. What happened was most of all what Agnes didn't want.

Patient-Directed Dying

Henry hung up the phone, raging inside, and then dropped to his knees crying. How could he, a lawyer, have allowed this to happen? Stella would blame him, he thought.

He rushed out of the office and hailed a taxi. When he got to the hospital he didn't know where to go, and he couldn't find the information desk. A nurse passing by sensed his despair and walked him to the emergency room. There, frantic, he had to wait at the front desk five or six minutes until a nurse came out.

"We can bring you back now, Mr. C." As they walked to the cubicle where Agnes lay on an emergency room bed, the nurse said, "I have to tell you, your wife is in critical condition. She's not breathing on her own, and I don't know if she'll make it, but the doctors have stabilized her on a mechanical respirator."

Through the open door of the room just ahead Henry could hear the whoosh-whoosh of the machine blowing air into and out of Agnes' lungs. He stopped, put his hands to his contorted face, and screamed. The nurse held his arm and led him into the room filled with machines and personnel hovering around the respirator, while bright overhead and portable lights shone down on Agnes, who lay motionless except when her whole body shook from each pulse of air emitted by the respirator.

"My God, my God, what have you done?" Henry groaned. Then he lurched over to the bed where he hugged Agnes as well as he could, given the tube down her throat. He pounded his fists on the bed, stood up fighting a torrent of tears, and addressed a white-coated doctor who stood next to the respirator with a stethoscope dangling around his neck.

"Why have you done this?" he implored.

"The medics did it. They had to—she had stopped breathing; she would have died. They did what they had to do."

"No, no." Henry lowered his head, and through his tears said, "She didn't want it—you're not supposed to have done that."

And then he fainted to the floor.

The emergency room personnel found Stella's cell phone number in Henry's wallet, called her, and she arrived, distraught, after racing across the mountains to Seattle. When she got to the hospital she found her father half asleep on a bed in the emergency room, fighting off a strong tranquilizer the nurse had insisted he take. Benjamin, the son from St. Louis, caught a late plane and arrived at the hospital about midnight.

Henry, Stella, and Benjamin went to see Agnes, who had been transferred to the intensive care unit and seemed to be unconscious. She did not respond to their presence. A few minutes later a young doctor entered, and after introductions he said no one could yet predict the outcome of the case, so the family might as well retire to the "family room" nearby. There they dropped into uncomfortable furniture across from a young man who snored intermittently.

The next morning, about 6:00 a.m., when a procession of carts wheeled noisily past the room, one by one they got up, went to the bathroom, and reassembled in the family room.

They had all looked in on Agnes, who lay immobile except for the intransigent pushes from the respirator, and Henry had gone into the room and stood beside Agnes's bed for a couple of minutes.

"I think she's awake. She looked at me," he reported to the others back in the family room.

"No," gasped Stella. She and Benjamin darted down the hall where Agnes's room was filled with nurses, doctors, and a technician who was telling the nurses about the settings on the breathing machine.

"Can you wait just a few minutes?" asked one of the nurses. "We'll be through and have her ready to see you in just a bit."

"Is she awake? Can she talk?" Benjamin asked.

"We don't think she's conscious, but she does move her eyes occasionally. She couldn't talk anyway, with the tube down her throat. Just wait in the family room, please." They withdrew as ordered.

Fifteen minutes later the nurse appeared in the family room. "You can go on in now. The doctors say that she's not conscious, but has some reflex movements of her eyes."

The three of them went down the hall together. In the room, Stella held Agnes's hand and wept softly. "Mother," she whispered.

"Mother," Benjamin shouted. There was no response.

"I guess I imagined she was awake," Henry said. "Maybe it's better this way, that she doesn't know what happened."

"I'm sure she's not feeling anything," the nurse said. "She's unconscious, and we're giving her intravenous morphine."

Henry, Stella, and Benjamin stayed with Agnes for at least half an hour before leaving to have breakfast in the hospital cafeteria. They ate silently. Then Henry spoke: "This is the last thing your mother would have wanted. We've got to make them take her off the respirator."

"I know it's not what she'd want," Stella said, "but it's happened, and you know she'll die if they do stop the lung machine."

"Yes, I know," Henry said, pushing down on his anger at Robb for calling the medics, and the entire medical system for what had happened. He looked at his children and said, "This is your mother up there hooked to that machine, and we're not going to allow it. We're going to do what she wants us to do."

"Yes, we'll do it," Stella said. And Benjamin repeated, "Yes, it's what Mother would want. Yes, we'll do it."

But it wasn't so easy to do. Agnes was still unconscious, or at least not responding under all the drugs she was getting, but the nurses and doctors said it was still possible she would recover. She was physically stable, and her blood pressure and oxygen levels were not as low as they had been the night before. The doctors were gaining ground—the numbers were better.

Later in the day the family met with the medical team members responsible for Agnes's care: a lung specialist, a cardiologist, and the head intensive-care doctor. They all seemed sympathetic, but before talking about anything else they insisted on going over—in detail—the medical facts of the case, which included a fifty-fifty chance that Agnes could recover enough to get off the ventilator. They had found a lot of fluid around the affected lung, and said that after draining it her breathing was easier, although she still needed mechanical assistance. She might regain consciousness, although during the time before the medics arrived, after Agnes had stopped breathing, she probably had sustained serious brain damage.

Finally Henry said, "Don't you know my wife has a living will saying she didn't want resuscitation, and most of all she wouldn't want to be on a breathing machine?"

The head doctor said yes, they had heard that Mrs. C. didn't want resuscitation, but they had no living will—they had nothing to support stopping any of the treatment. After more discussion about Agnes's statements about not wanting to be on a ventilator, the meeting ended by the doctor saying he had to consult with the hospital's medical director and attorneys, and he asked Henry to get a copy of Agnes's living will.

Stella and Benjamin went to their parents' home, got the living will and DNR form, and brought it back to the hospital where the head intensive-care doctor looked at it.

"Let's meet tomorrow, at 9:00 a.m.," he said.

The next morning the head doctor said he had checked with the medical director and the hospital attorney, and the request was in order. "When do you want us to do this?" he asked.

"Might as well do it now, or this afternoon," Henry said.

Who Decides?—The Story of Agnes

"Let's wait until tomorrow," Stella said. "It'll give us some time to be ready for it." The others looked at her, said nothing, and nodded assent.

"I think tomorrow is best," the doctor said. "We'll have everything ready at 9:00 a.m.

When the family gathered in the waiting room the next day at 9:00 a.m., the doctor suggested they go to Agnes' room to say their last good-byes. Agnes was the same, lifeless except for her chest moving up with each push from the respirator. They all hugged her, whispered their good-byes, and then retired to the waiting room—to wait.

In about half an hour the head doctor appeared and said, "Everything went smoothly."

PART III
Going Forward

Throughout the Nation, Americans are engaged in an earnest and profound debate about the morality, legality, and practicality of physician-assisted suicide. Our holding permits this debate to continue, as it should in a democratic society.

—U.S. Supreme Court Chief Justice Rehnquist[36]

I do not, however, foreclose the possibility that an individual plaintiff seeking to hasten her death, or a doctor whose assistance was sought, could prevail in a more particularized challenge.

—U.S. Supreme Court Justice Stevens[37]

Chapter 6

GOING FORWARD

Mercy Doesn't Kill

How should we proceed in order to make patient-directed aid in dying legal and accessible? We face a paradox: the majority of people in this country want a legal means of helping terminally ill patients die,[38] but except for the success in Oregon, "death-with-dignity" ballot measures or initiatives on aid in dying have failed in those states where it's been voted upon: California, Washington, Michigan, and Maine. Most proponents feel these defeats reflect social conservatives' well-funded efforts to frighten voters by predicting "killing" and a "culture of death," and politicians' avoidance of this "hot-button" issue because open support might lose them re-election votes.

We have much work to do, for we face lawmakers, judges, and an electorate largely uninformed about how we die. We must educate everyone about the myths and false propositions that obstruct their understanding of the realities and rightness of self-determination for terminally ill patients.[39] We must inform the public about the dying process and the role of physicians and medical technology in determining how we die. We must help them understand how the concept of "sanctity of life" has expanded over time so that now it includes—incorrectly, I believe—biological life that is created or distorted by medical technology. We must help people understand that ending artificially prolonged life is neither suicide nor a violation of "the will of God." And we must help dying patients and their families to urge their physicians to overcome the ancient taboo against helping their patients die.

We need to help people understand that patient-directed aid in dying is *not* killing, ethically or legally, and will result in less abuse and better end-of-life care for all patients than now occurs. We need to help people understand that to have a physician write a prescription for a lethal dose of medicine is not a radical break from other end-of-life medical practices that are already widespread and ethically and legally acceptable—for example, withdrawing life-support therapy or administering palliative sedation. In all three practices patients do not die "naturally," the underlying disease is the true cause of death, and the medical act is the last in a long series of interventions controlling the dying process. Abuse under open and legalized aid in dying is less likely than occurs privately with withdrawing life-support therapy or with palliative sedation.

We need to be very clear about our goal: aid in dying for the terminally ill is an *option*, not a policy. I remember well a symposium on physician-aided dying held by a national hospice organization a few years ago. I was the advocate, and the opponent spoke first. He began by pointing to me and saying to the assembled hospice personnel: "Make no mistake, he wants your patients, and if he and others like him get his way, they will kill your patients instead of letting them join your hospices." Wow! Heavy stuff! I was so shocked and dumbfounded I could scarcely respond.

It took me years to understand why some people, speaking with conviction, would make such a charge. Now I realize it's because they believe that legalized aid in dying would be tantamount to *promoting* or advocating the practice for everyone. This, they believe, would result in government-sanctioned killing through public policy.

Honest fear lay beneath my symposium opponent's otherwise irrational charge. Because he and similar-minded opponents seek to prevent *anyone* from using aid in dying, they presume that supporters are equally absolutist about advocating their position and thus would try to enlist or coerce *everyone* to die with their physicians' help if and when it became legal to do so. We must dispel this irrational notion. An option for a terminally ill patient to die with lethal medicine would be no more likely to become public policy than the option for withdrawing life-sustaining treatment, or palliative sedation. Nor is there a shred of evidence from Oregon that the option has become or is likely to become a policy.[40]

The potential for abuse of the disabled is a concern for both proponents and opponents of aid in dying because of disabled people's vulnerability to discrimination and their sense of being devalued by nondisabled people. While some disabled people vocally oppose legalizing aid in dying, they are in the minority on this issue.[41]

Going Forward

Their argument is that once the act became legal for those with terminal illnesses, logic and "fairness" would mandate its availability to anyone with an incurable illness or condition. Under this line of reasoning, since disabled patients are by medical definition "abnormal," in due time society would bring pressure to bear on all disabled patients to end their lives. They fear it would become a policy, not an option. While it is easy to understand their profound anxieties and fears, these fears do not stand up to scrutiny.

There is no evidence of abuse of disabled patients who are dependent on life-supporting treatment, for whom withdrawing essential treatment can be done more easily and less voluntarily than would be the case with aid in dying. In Oregon, and under all proposals in other states, legalized aid in dying requires certification that the patient is terminally ill, mandates a waiting time after the patient's first request for it, and requires adequate palliative care and mental health assessment if depression is suspected. These are all safeguards that are not in place for withdrawing life-sustaining treatment from dying patients.

The extreme sensitivity of disabled persons to potential abuse and the political and legal ramifications for abusers of disabled persons make it less likely to happen to them than perhaps to any other segment of our society. Physicians are excessively aware of potential liability in dealing with disabled persons. The mere suspicion of the involuntary death of a disabled person, under the guise of patient-directed aid in dying, would overwhelm the defense of an innocent physician in a wrongful death court case.

Patient-Directed Dying

One may on religious or ideological grounds deny the moral equivalence of patient-directed dying to other forms of aid in dying such as palliative sedation or disconnecting a ventilator, but there is no practical difference. The outcome—death—is the same, and none of these acts are suicide.

Mercy doesn't kill people. It is incorrect for anyone to say that a physician's intent in complying with a patient's request for a large dose of sleeping pills is to "kill." Yes, any physician knows that death will occur if his patient takes a lethal dose of pills he has prescribed. But *knowing* what might happen is not the same as wanting or *intending* it. If it were, then *knowing* that administering palliative sedation or withdrawing a ventilator will cause death is the same as *intending* it, and so these practices also would constitute "killing."

A physician knows that disconnecting a ventilator will cause death for a patient dependent on it; can we say he does not intend what he knows will happen? His best and basic intention is to act in accordance with the patient's request to act so as to relieve suffering. But can we say he does not intend to cause death when he knows it will happen, or wishes it wouldn't? It is the same with aid in dying: the true and primary intent of prescribing lethal pills is to relieve suffering if the patient chooses to use the pills for that reason. The physician who in this manner enables his patient's death does not intend the death as a matter of desire—he intends relief of suffering.

Furthermore, in giving a prescription for lethal drugs to a dying patient who has requested it, a physician does not know with certainty that death will result since more than a third of

Going Forward

the patients who obtain the drugs do not ultimately use them.[42] In contrast, a physician who withdraws life-sustaining therapy *knows* with much greater certainty that death will follow from the act. And a physician who administers palliative sedation *knows* with certainty that death will result from that act. Can a physician do something that he knows will cause death without actually intending the death? It is a question for Socrates, but whatever the answer, the judgment should be the same for all three procedures.

In aid in dying, death depends on the will of the patient: it is patient-directed. Precisely because the death-causing act is the patient's, not the physician's, abuse is less likely to occur than with sanctioned withdrawal of life-support or palliative sedation.

Terminally ill patients should be allowed to choose their mode of dying.

Supremely Backward

Does aid in dying violate state interests? States have a legitimate interest in preserving life by preventing negligence, murder, and ordinary suicide. If an act is called suicide, it follows that assisting the act would violate the presumed state interest. But when the state antisuicide laws were enacted 150 years ago no one had in mind a dying patient whose life had been medically and artificially extended to a condition of prolonged suffering.

Key questions not adequately addressed or answered by the U.S. Supreme Court are: Should the state interest in preserving life be so absolute as to condemn patients to unnatural, medically-managed dying with extended suffering? Is this a legitimate state function? Does the state have an interest in eking a few weeks or months of life out of dying patients who will succumb to their diseases within a few weeks or months? Should the state interest be to preserve life by prolonging it at all costs, by unnatural means, or should the state interest be in promoting the interest of the dying patient? Should the state disallow aid in dying when it allows physicians to shorten the lives of far greater numbers of patients by withdrawing life-sustaining treatments or by administering morphine drips or palliative sedation?

Does the traditional state interest in preventing suicide apply to patients who are dying? If so, why is it indiscriminately applied to patients who take pills and not to patients who direct their physicians to withdraw life-sustaining therapy or sedate them continuously until they die? What about patients who choose not to prolong their lives by months or years and refuse chemotherapy or extensive surgery—should state interest mandate them to accept the treatments? If the state interest is in preserving all human life as long as possible, should we mandate maximum curative therapy for everyone right up to the moment of death? Why does the state single out one of many different terminally ill groups of patients for maximally prolonged life?

What about the legal "tradition" against suicide in this country? Tradition carries much weight with the law, but sometimes it serves to defend and sustain unworthy social attitudes and practices. Racial segregation had a long legal tradition in this country, but it wasn't right. Legal tradition supported male-only suffrage for ages—that didn't make it right. Most importantly, the legal tradition against suicide in this country arose from a concern about non-dying people. When the tradition of "suicide" is incorrectly applied to terminally ill patients it promotes prolonged dying and suffering. Is this a state interest?

At what point should the state's interest in prolonging life cease? Take the case of Mary W., a woman diagnosed with breast cancer ten years ago, who had extensive surgery followed by a full course of chemotherapy and then intermittent chemotherapy for the next nine years. She now has been bedridden for a year, has some breakthrough pain and severe constipation despite excellent overall comfort care by her hospice team, and she asks to die. Beyond question, her life has been extended by years, but now it offers her only misery. What is the state's interest in keeping Mary alive if she voluntarily requests to end her life? Is it to conform to the sanctity-of-life principle and to prolong life as much as possible? Is it to protect the "integrity" of the state medical society?

The paramount state interest should be in promoting compassion for and reducing the suffering of dying patients.

The Turning Point—Terminal Illness

I believe that when a patient becomes terminally ill—when life has been preserved and prolonged through medical therapy up to the point where further medical treatments are *ineffective* in restoring health or preserving meaningful life—

the state's interest in preserving or prolonging life has been met. It has been more than met since, with rare exceptions, every patient with a terminal illness has had medical treatment for the underlying disease and has had his or her life extended or prolonged beyond the point of natural death. *The state interest should be to prolong life only so long as doing so doesn't harm the patient*, not for as long as is technically possible.

Except for people who die quickly or suddenly without medical treatments, everyone who is terminally ill has had prior medical life extension. Take the example of George H., age 54, who had acute leukemia with a probability of about 5 percent for surviving five years after diagnosis, even with therapy. He might have forgone therapy and died within a few months. Instead, he had chemotherapy and advanced radiation therapy that prolonged his life by at least three years. When he reached the point of having no realistic chance of living longer with more curative therapy, he had more than met any legitimate state interest in preserving or prolonging life.

What could the state gain by insisting that George prolong his life as much as possible with all available treatments, and with continued suffering? If a patient is suffering and wants to die at this point, the interest of the state should shift and become his—the patient's interest. There should be no state interest in deterring any form of aid in dying for a patient like George who has met the condition of prolonging his life for as long as possible and who now wishes to die to avoid further suffering.

Patient-directed aid in dying will serve the state's interest by improving the care of *all* dying patients. As we have noted, since legalization of aid in dying in Oregon, a higher percentage of all its terminally ill patients have enrolled in hospice plans than in any other state, and aggressive palliative care has also increased dramatically.

Who's Dying, Anyway?

U.S. Supreme Court Chief Justice Rehnquist wrote, in *Washington v. Glucksberg*, "The State also has an interest in protecting the integrity and ethics of the medical profession....Physician-assisted suicide could, it is argued, undermine the trust that is essential to the doctor-patient relationship by blurring the time-honored line between healing and harming."[43]

The Court here assumes that keeping a dying patient alive is healing, while giving him or her the means to die is harming. I believe the Court got it backwards. Much harm is done by insisting that dying patients live as long as possible, while on the other hand giving a terminally ill patient the means of dying actually relieves suffering.

The Court seemed more interested in the opinion of the American Medical Association than the concerns of dying patients, noting that the AMA opposed legalized aid in dying. But why should the highest court in the land so readily support a medical society that speaks for less than half of American physicians? And even if the AMA represented the majority opinion of the country's physicians, which it does not, why should the Court support the medical profession instead of dying patients?[44] Furthermore, national and state polls over the last 10 years show that a majority or a plurality of the entire medical profession supports patient-directed dying within guidelines.[45]

Of course, all states have a legitimate interest in the well-being of their professions and their practitioners. But who's dying, anyway? Whose integrity do we need to preserve? Is the medical profession dying? What about the integrity of dying patients? The state's ultimate interest in the integrity of its professions shouldn't be that they serve themselves, but that they serve the public. Would we ask any less of the legal profession?

The dictum "physicians must cure, not kill" also affected the Supreme Court's reasoning in opposing aid in dying.[46] Yet an overemphasis on curing, when carried on to the bitter end and beyond reasonable likelihood of success, is more likely to undermine the public's trust in the medical profession because it prolongs the dying process and preempts the comfort care terminally ill patients need. As Justice Stevens wrote in a separate opinion, "For some patients, it would be a physician's refusal to dispense medication to ease their suffering and make their death tolerable and dignified that would be inconsistent with the healing role."[47] When curative therapy becomes ineffective for a dying patient, doctors must learn to place their duty to relieve human suffering above their responsibility to prolong life.

GOING FORWARD

If patient-directed dying would harm the integrity of the medical profession, one wonders why a majority of physicians want the option of directing their own dying.[48]

Changing state laws may be our best, and only, road to obtaining legal assistance in dying. The U.S. Supreme Court, in its decisions in both *Glucksberg* and *Quill*, went no further than to say that state laws banning aid in dying are not unconstitutional; they did not say that a law allowing it would be unconstitutional. Justice Souter noted the "superior opportunity" of legislatures "to obtain the facts necessary for a judgment," and to experiment as facts emerge.[49] The Court felt that state legislatures were better suited to debate and resolve this difficult societal issue. They passed the buck back to the states.

The legislative arena might seem to be the more democratic forum for establishing laws, but it is also a highly political arena and one that is most susceptible to pressure from special-interest groups like anti-abortion and "right-to-life" groups. Although more Americans approve than disapprove of patient-directed dying, to date no state legislature has enacted this preference into legislation. To wit, in a general election voters approved the Oregon Death with Dignity Act, allowing aid in dying. The Oregon legislature then defied the public will by nullifying the vote, but in a second vote the Oregon electorate reapproved the Death with Dignity Act by an even greater margin than in the first vote. Surely, this was not the example Justice Souter had in mind when he noted the "superior opportunity" of legislatures "to obtain the facts necessary for a judgment," and to experiment as facts emerge. In our democracy, why do we let the minority block the wish of the majority?

The political calculus at present in state legislatures may not be favorable for legislation like in Oregon, but this is where our efforts must go. And there are encouraging developments. The Hawaii legislature came very close to approving a law similar to Oregon's—it passed both houses but was not enacted when two senators were persuaded to change their minds. Vermont is active in moving legislation to allow aid in dying, and California legislators are also working on a similar bill. Winning approval in state legislatures will be difficult, but the winds of change are blowing.

Privatize Dying!

If we can privatize our public utilities, our schools, and even Social Security, why shouldn't we privatize the most individual and private function we will all face—dying? Get the government out of the death bedroom. Many don't want the government to say how we must tax a dying patient's estate; why do they allow the government to say how a person can or cannot die?

To have no law on the subject is one approach to aid in dying. And although many physicians are either firmly for or against legalizing aid in dying and would like the law to reflect their views, even more would prefer no law at all governing it.[50] In a survey from Michigan, 40 percent of physicians preferred legalizing "physician-assisted suicide" and 17 percent favored prohibition, while 37 percent preferred "no law," i.e., no government regulation.[51] In general, physicians prefer to be left alone to practice as they see fit.

In 1994 I wrote an op-ed piece for *The New York Times* in which I pointed out the widespread and unregulated practice of "morphine drips," used in hospitals to help dying patients.[52] Although I realized the article might rankle some physicians, I was unprepared for physicians of all types and ideologies criticizing me for writing openly about morphine drips. One busy surgeon stopped me in a hospital corridor and said, glowering, "There are some things in medicine we must just do, and we shouldn't discuss them publicly."

Most physicians believe that medical decisions and practices are intensely private matters into which the state should not intrude. Because physicians believe they know what is best for their patients, they fear that regulation would limit patient options and subvert optimal patient care; they don't want government telling them how to practice medicine.

Some physicians who oppose legalizing aid in dying nevertheless condone or even advocate acting outside the law if there is a compelling medical or ethical reason to do so. They will admit to having had so-called "heart-wrenching" cases in which patients would be best served if they were helped to die. A physician friend of mine who is an outspoken opponent of legalizing aid in dying told me how, on rare occasions, he covertly euthanizes his dying patients who are incurable and approaching a time of great suffering.

The author and surgeon Sherwin Nuland, who does not favor legalized aid in dying, wrote: "If the fully informed person whose suffering I cannot relieve repeatedly asks that I aid him in his determination to end his life, whether by pill or injection, I am obligated to do so. A tolerant society should allow it."[53] He defends the practice of helping a patient die as consistent with the ideal of the Hippocratic Oath, which urges physicians to act always for "the benefit of the sick." But, like many physicians, Nuland distinguishes between what he thinks is best for all physicians in general, and what he thinks an individual physician should do on a rare occasion. Of course, with this approach the physician, not the patient, makes the decision.

Not a few members of the legal profession also have objected to legalization of aid in dying, while wanting to have the option available for themselves or those who need it. I once told a lawyer who has worked doggedly to oppose legalized aid in dying that I did not wish to break the law in helping patients die. Half in jest he grabbed me by the shirt, but said earnestly, "If you have a patient suffering miserably who needs to die, and you don't help him die, you are a bad doctor." He made it clear that, if necessary, I should circumvent the law to help patients die, whatever the risk.

For many years a noted lawyer chaired the American Bar Association Commission on Legal Problems of the Elderly, during which time he successfully led the opposition to a resolution supporting legal "physician-assisted suicide." Nevertheless, in an article he wrote outlining his opposition, he said: "At the same time I selfishly reserve my right to do in private what my family, my doctor and pastor and I, in loving consultation, voluntarily agree is best."[54]

Going Forward

How does one reconcile these contradictions? Are these opponents practicing a double standard? Well, yes, they are. But jurists know that some laws should occasionally be broken in extreme or needy cases—a driver taking a heart attack victim to a hospital should exceed the speed limit in an effort to save the person's life, for example. In the same way, we need exceptions to meet needs of patients that laws against aid in dying otherwise would not permit.[55] Other jurists dispute the wisdom of undermining respect for the law by reserving the option of doing privately what one opposes in public. These diverse opinions reflect our society's ambivalence over this vexing issue.

Unfortunately, the legal status of aid in dying has substantial impact on access to it, and on attitudes of physicians and the general public toward it. In my opinion, an attitude that permits patient-directed dying outside the law for individuals who have the wherewithal and resources to gain access to it, yet bans it for others, discriminates among dying patients: privileged patients can skirt the law and avoid excessive suffering at the end of life, while the less fortunate others must endure prolonged suffering. We must rectify this inequality.

The standard for statutory regulation of how physicians may help patients die should be prohibition of wrongful killing, not helping terminally ill patients die peacefully.

Since even many opponents acknowledge a need for exceptions to the law for patients dying in extreme agony, a solution within the present laws to allow aid in dying in compelling cases probably would be welcome to a large majority of the public.

The U.S. Supreme Court may have provided a legal opening to such a compromise. Chief Justice Rehnquist, in delivering the opinion of the Court in *Glucksberg* and *Quill*, quoted approvingly from a report of a New York state task force: "It is widely recognized that the provision of pain medication is ethically and professionally acceptable even when the treatment may hasten the patient's death, if the medication is intended to alleviate pain and severe discomfort, not to cause death,"[56] and in a concurring opinion Justice Stevens wrote: "A doctor who prescribes lethal medication does not necessarily intend the patient's death—rather that doctor may seek simply to ease the patient's suffering and to comply with her wishes."[57] These interpretations may point the way to legitimate and acceptable uses of patient-directed dying in cases previously held to be exceptions to the general rule. Also, they would be consistent with society's time-honored practice of using new interpretations to make a medical practice conform to the sanctity-of-life principle.

From these statements one would conclude that if a physician's primary intent is to relieve pain or suffering, he may prescribe drugs that might hasten the dying of a terminally ill patient. If true, physicians therefore can and should become more aggressive with palliative care, and should be prescribing larger doses of painkillers or sedatives to relieve end-of-life suffering even if they caused earlier deaths for some patients. George Annas, a noted legal scholar and forceful opponent of legalizing aid in dying, gives his interpretation of what a physician may do within the law:

"Providing terminally ill patients with drugs they might use to kill themselves does not currently constitute assisted suicide, even if the patient actually uses them for suicide, unless it is the physician's intent that the patient so use them. Physicians legally can, and as a matter of good medical practice should, supply prescriptions for potentially lethal drugs that have a legitimate medical use to their terminally ill patients on request, if they believe that having these drugs is likely to permit the patient to live better." [58]

This interpretation applies the "double effect" principle to the prescribing of drugs that, taken all at once, are lethal (the intended effect is relief of suffering while a foreseen but unintended effect may be death). We know from studies of dying patients that those who acquire lethal quantities of medicines have an increased sense of well-being and less fear of dying precisely because they have the option of ending their lives. Also, they are less likely to end their lives prematurely, particularly by violent means.[59] The pills are a dying patient's security blanket.

The immediate and major disadvantage of this approach is its impracticality. Physicians are not social pioneers. No amount of brilliant legal discourse can convince most physicians to take legal or professional risks until many others have taken the same risks without prosecution. If the U.S. Justice Department succeeds in its attempt to place all prescribing of potent painkillers and sedatives under the scrutiny of federal agents, with threats of punishment for prescribing morphine for dying patients, doctors will become like heretics brought before the grand inquisitor.[60]

Physicians who heed the pleas of their patients to help them die in private must act outside the law (except in Oregon)—and, importantly, outside the scrutiny of peers or state regulation. If patient-directed dying were legal, it would be out in the open and regulated, and continuously reassessed to be sure it serves patients well and does not foster abuses.

Establishing legal and professional precedence for privacy in dying within the present state laws would have the advantage of giving regulated access to patient-directed aid in dying for those who want it and qualify for it, without physicians having to fear prosecution or the intrusion of governmental regulation. It would also have the advantage for opponents of maintaining the law against aid in dying, which for them is culturally important.

A compromise possibly acceptable to both sides of the aid in dying conflict would be to change the law to allow verifiable exceptions while maintaining the overall prohibition. That is, aid in dying would remain illegal but the new law would recognize exceptions and permit physicians to perform it if done within guidelines.[61]

Guidelines would follow the requirements set forth in the Oregon law which specify that patients must be terminally ill adults; must have access to adequate palliative care; must be making a voluntary request without undue coercion and consistent with the patient's values and goals; must not be clinically depressed; must make at least two formal requests with a waiting period between them; and the decision must not be made for economic purposes. A physician who prescribed a lethal dose of medicine, which his patient then used to die, would have an "affirmative" legal defense against criminal charges of assistance in dying, and would be granted immunity from the law if he met the stated guidelines.

There are several advantages to this approach. For opponents of legalizing aid in dying it should be comforting to keep in place a law consistent with the principle that suicide is wrong, although the law would make the distinction between suicide and the ending of life of a terminally ill patient. The law would retain criminal sanctions for physicians who inappropriately or abusively helped patients die, thereby protecting vulnerable patients as well as or better than the present laws. It would diminish the threat of prosecution of physicians and protect those who act within the guidelines, while maintaining the privacy of physicians, patients, and families without the bureaucratic intrusions of governmental oversight. In short, it would provide for "privacy in dying" while maintaining the prohibition against killing patients (euthanasia or coerced aid in dying).[62]

The Future of Dying

In the future, instead of enduring just one terminal illness people will experience the early stages of a succession of multiple dying processes, each in turn cured or slowed by advanced technology. The elderly will lurch toward senility and/or overwhelming physical disability. Humans will share

Patient-Directed Dying

the fate of the Struldbrugs, a race of people Gulliver encountered on the island of Luggnagg. The Struldbrugs lived forever and, as Gulliver noted, "Besides the usual deformities in extreme old age, they acquired an additional ghastliness in proportion to their years." They had no pleasure, and whenever they saw a funeral they pined that they also could be laid to rest.[63]

What will be our fate if more than half our citizens survive longer than 100–110 years? We may become a society of miserable, suffering Struldbrugs, enfeebled and unable to escape ever-longer life. For those suspended in the half cure of artificial life, the human dilemma has already become deciding when and how to quit life. Slowly dying patients deserve and need a socially and legally acceptable means of ending their dying processes when medical treatments no longer offer a reasonable chance of meaningful or functional life.

Our old attitudes are not appropriate to the new conditions of dying. A law that forces a patient to endure what he considers to be an odious end to his dying process represents a misuse of power. In the future we must judge the *entire* medically managed process of dying—the process of first extending life and then helping to end it. Only then can we assess whether the process was ethical or unethical, appropriate or inappropriate.

Helping suffering people die does not mean disrespecting or repudiating the most important ethical principle and protection we have: the principle of the sanctity of life. Respect or reverence for life should remain the keystone of our legal and medical systems. But we must reexamine the meaning of

Going Forward

"sanctity of life" when life no longer serves its natural function. Society is not justified in maintaining laws that disrespect and harm a person by not allowing her to die when, in accordance with her spiritual values and beliefs, her life has become dehumanized and desanctified. When a terminally ill person's religious beliefs lead him to conclude that he has allowed his life to become contrary to the purpose of his God, he should have the religious freedom to sanctify good life by ending his life of degradation. In our free society we dare not use the law to enforce on everyone a particular world view of the meaning of life and death. We must resist use of the sanctity-of-life principle to further individual or institutional causes.

We should respect life always, and sanctify it to its natural end, but when death becomes more natural than life we should have no obligation to sanctify a life that has been medically transformed into something alien and unnatural. Doing so will harm the sanctity-of-life principle itself.

We must understand death as part of the human condition and accept it when continued existence defiles natural life. *We must acquire respect for the sanctity of death.*

We have all, physicians and patients, trapped ourselves in a technological-moral morass by not acknowledging our human hand in putting patients into unnaturally extended dying processes. And we as a society have deferred to a medical profession that has not adapted to the consequences of its own technology and is too often profession-centered rather than patient-centered. When we have made life artificial and harmful for a person who is suffering with a terminal illness

Patient-Directed Dying

and does not wish to continue life, we must allow patient-directed aid in dying.

APPENDIX

THE OREGON DEATH WITH DIGNITY ACT (DWDA)

The DWDA was passed by voters in 1994 and became law after being reaffirmed in 1997. It:

* Allows qualified patients suffering from a terminal disease to voluntarily request a prescription for medication to end his or her life.
* Allows the patient to rescind his or her request at any time or in any manner.
* Allows doctors, pharmacists and other health care providers to refuse to participate.
* Allows the patient's family and physician to be present at the time the patient takes the medication.
* Does not allow lethal injection, or euthanasia.
* The patient must be an adult, 18 years of age or older, must have a terminal illness with less than 6 months to live, and must make a voluntary request.
* The patient must be a resident of Oregon to participate.
* A physician not licensed in Oregon cannot participate.
* Requires a 15-day waiting period after an oral request for a prescription for medication to end life.
* Doesn't specify which medication may be used.

The Oregon Death With Dignity Act (DWDA)

* The patient must be informed of options, including pain and comfort care, and hospice care.
* The attending physician is to determine that the patient is capable of making his or her own health care decisions and is acting voluntarily.
* The attending physician is to ask (but can't require) the patient to notify next of kin of his or her decision.
* The patient must be referred to a consulting physician for a second opinion, to verify the attending physician's diagnosis and prognosis, and whether the patient is capable of making his or her own health care decisions and is acting voluntarily.
* If either the attending physician or consulting physician believes the patient is suffering from a psychiatric or psychological illness or depression causing impaired judgment, the patient must be referred for counseling.
* The attending physician and the consulting physician must document in the patient's chart the diagnosis, prognosis, potential risks associated with taking the medication, result of taking the medication, and feasible alternatives, which include but are not limited to comfort care, hospice, and symptom control.
* Once the preceding steps have been satisfied, the patient voluntarily signs a written request witnessed by two people, at least one of whom is not a relative or an heir.
* The patient must then restate his oral request for medication.

Patient-Directed Dying

* No sooner than 15 days after the initial oral request and 48 hours after the written request, the patient may receive a prescription for medication to end his or her life.
* After a prescription is written, forms for the attending physician, the consulting physician, the patient's written request for medication, and, if obtained, the psychiatric/psychological consultant's form must be filled out and sent to the Oregon Health Division.
* The Health Division annually reviews a sample of records.

For annual report from the Oregon Department of Health, see: www.oregon.gov/DHS/ph/pas

GLOSSARY

<u>Active Euthanasia</u>. Same as euthanasia. Implies consent of the patient. See passive euthanasia.

<u>Aid in Dying</u>. Although this is a generic term referring to any means of helping a patient die, in this book I use it to mean the act whereby a terminally ill patient directs his or her dying, enabled by a physician who assists by writing a prescription for a lethal dose of medicine.

<u>Assisted Dying</u>. A generic term that means much the same as Aid in Dying. Some proponents use this term exclusively for aid in dying.

<u>Assisted Suicide</u>. The act of assisting someone who *initiates* dying and ends his/her own life. The term is incorrect if used for a terminally ill patient. See physician-assisted suicide.

<u>Clinical Depression</u>. Depression that is internal to the patient and is not due to a transient external or adverse life event. Also called *major* depression. See "situational" depression.

Glossary

Comfort Care. A general term for relief of physical or emotional suffering; can be applied to any patient, including but not restricted to those who are terminally ill. Commonly refers to pain control. See palliative sedation.

Death. The end of the process of dying; the cessation of life.

Dying. A process beginning with an ultimately fatal illness, and ending at the time of death. In modern times this process is modified by medical interventions unless a person dies suddenly or with no medical care.

Double Effect. An ethical principle applied to a medical act that has two effects: the first effect is intended as beneficial to the patient, e.g., a drug given for relief of suffering; a second possible unintended but foreseen and harmful effect is death from the act, e.g., an administered drug such as morphine.

Euthanasia. Literally means "peaceful dying." As used in reference to dying patients, it means an act taken by another that ends the life of the patient, such as a physician administering a lethal drug. Although often not specified, the term implies voluntariness or consent of the patient to the act. Often called active euthanasia. Euthanasia without the consent of the patient is involuntary euthanasia.

Hastened Dying. This generic term is most commonly used to mean patient-directed dying. Less commonly, or rarely, it is used to refer to any means of ending life more quickly than with routine medical and palliative care, and is similar in meaning to aid in dying.

Hospice. An organization or medical plan emphasizing quality of life for dying patients rather than further attempts with curative therapy. See "hospice care."

Hospice Care. The practice of maximizing quality of life of terminally ill patients through palliative care and avoidance or prohibition of curative or life-prolonging measures. In the United States most patients in hospice plans are cared for in their homes, but some hospices have "in-patient" facilities.

Morphine Drip. An intravenous or subcutaneous (beneath the skin) treatment with morphine or a similar narcotic drug, or sedative. Doctors commonly use this method to relieve pain after operations or other medical emergencies. It is also used for cancer patients to treat pain that is too severe to be adequately controlled with pills or patches. Although this form of treatment with morphine is safe even for dying patients, at higher doses it can cause sedation or unconsciousness. If the dose is increased above safe levels it can cause death.

Palliative Care. Provision of drugs or other treatments to control or address physical or psychological suffering; similar to comfort care. Refers primarily to relief of physical suffering—the skills that physicians use to relieve suffering and improve quality of life. Palliative care is not the absence or

GLOSSARY

withdrawal of medical care, but when used in the context of hospice care commonly implies absence of curative treatments. See comfort care.

Palliative Sedation (also called continuous sedation or terminal sedation). The continuous use of a sedative to render a patient unconscious for the purpose of relieving extreme physical distress or suffering. Although sedation to relieve physical suffering is used for non-dying patients (e.g., following surgery) when referred to as *palliative* sedation, it is for patients who are dying and have no prospect of recovery, and is accompanied by withholding or withdrawal of food and liquids until the patient dies.

Passive Euthanasia. An ambiguous term sometimes used to describe withdrawal of life-sustaining treatment, such as an artificial ventilator. Often used to mean aid in dying that is not direct or active euthanasia. See active euthanasia.

Patient-Directed Dying. *Assisted Dying,* from the perspective of the patient. It is the voluntary death of a terminally ill patient by self-administration of a lethal amount of drug or agent. Replaces the anachronistic term "physician-assisted suicide" which is inadequate to describe the condition and purpose of the dying patient.

Physician-Enabled Dying. *Assisted Dying,* from the perspective of the physician. Assistance by a physician in making available a lethal amount of a drug or agent to a terminally ill patient who uses it to end his/her own life. The patient self-administers the lethal drug or agent. If a physician or anyone else administers the drug the act is euthanasia.

Physician-Assisted Suicide (PAS). Inaccurate term, replaced in this book by patient-directed dying, or aid in dying.

Situational Depression. Sometimes called "reactive" depression. Reaction to an external and severe life event such as loss of job or death of a spouse. Not typical of the person's usual response to stress, and can be a normal reaction to the event. Often a reaction to one's own impending death.

Suicide. The taking of one's own life by a person who has a treatable or controllable condition and is not terminally ill or otherwise dying. The suicidal person initiates the dying process. This word does not apply to the act of patient-directed dying.

Sanctity of Life. The principle that all life is sanctified or holy, as given by God. Usually applies only to human life.

Terminally Ill. Implies a patient with an incurable disease who is dying with less than six months to live (by best medical judgment). Generally used as criterion for admission to a hospice plan.

READINGS

BOOKS

D. W. Amundsen, *Medicine, Society, and Faith in the Ancient and Modern Worlds* (The Johns Hopkins University Press, Baltimore, 1996).

M. P. Battin, *The Least Worst Death* (Oxford University Press, New York, 1994).

D. Callahan, *The Troubled Dream of Life* (Simon & Schuster, New York, 1993).

P. Carick, *Medical Ethics in the Ancient World* (Georgetown University Press, Washington DC, 2001).

G. Dworkin, R.G. Frey, and S.Bok, *Euthanasia and Physician-Assisted Suicide. For and Against* (Cambridge University Press, Cambridge, U.K., 1998).

M. J. Field and C. K. Cassel, Editors. *Approaching Death. Improving Care at the End of Life* (National Academy Press: Washington DC, 1997).

Readings

K. Foley and H. Hendin, Editors. *The Case Against Assisted Suicide* (The Johns Hopkins University Press, Baltimore, 2002).

G.E. Lloyd, Ed. *Hippocratic Writings* (Penguin Books, London, 1983).

C. F. McKhann, *A Time to Die* (Yale University Press, New Haven, 1999).

T. A. Preston, *Final Victory* (Forum, Roseville, CA, 2000).

T. E. Quill and Battin, M. P., editors. *Physician-Assisted Dying. The Case for Palliative Care & Patient Choice* (The Johns Hopkins University Press, Baltimore, 2004).

Supreme Court of the United States. Nos. 96–110 and 95-1858, June 26, 1997.

O. Temkin, "The Idea of the Respect for Life in the History of Medicine." In, *Respect for Life in Medicine, Philosophy, and the Law*, O. Temkin, W. K. Frankena, and S. H. Kadish (The Johns Hopkins University Press, Baltimore, 1977).

O. Temkin, *Hippocrates in a World of Pagans and Christians* (The Johns Hopkins University Press, Baltimore, 1991).

M. Webb, *The Good Death* (Bantam Books, New York, 1997).

When Death is Sought: Assisted Dying and Euthanasia in the Medical Context (New York State Task Force on Life and the Law, 1994).

WEB SITES

www.dying.about.com
About's complete site dedicated to death, dying, terminal illness, funerals, euthanasia, hospice, grief, bereavement and pet loss. Every aspect of death.

http://www.growthhouse.org
Resources for life-threatening illness, end of life care, bereavement and grief, death and dying.

www.nhpco.org
Charitable organization created in 1992 to broaden America's understanding of hospice through research and education. Includes a directory of hospice care,…

www.HospiceCare.com
Info about hospice & palliative care services.

www.hospicenet.org/pain control: dispelling the myths · helping yourself live while dying…preparing for approaching death · helping a friend who is dying.

www.death-and-dying.org/
Buddhist insights into death and dying.

Readings

www.buddhanet.net/bereaved.htm
Directory; caring for the dying & bereaved; funeral rites for the dead; download articles and ebooks on death & dying; HIV/AIDS prevention and care…

www.elisabethkublerross.com
Elizabeth Kubler Ross. Author of *On Death & Dying* website books, news, videos and grief info.

www.religioustolerance.org/euthanas.htm
A thorough site with varying perspectives on the right to die, public opinion polls, and religious beliefs about hastened dying.

www.wings.buffalo.edu/faculty/research/bioethics/court.html
Annotated legal cases on physician-assisted suicide in the USA, 89 pp. US Supreme Court rules on physician assisted suicide cases…

www.oregon.gov/DHS/ph/pas
Oregon Death with Dignity Law

www.ohd.hr.state.or.us/chs/pas/pas.cfm
Full text of measure passed by Oregon voters in which doctors assist terminally ill patients with dying.

www.oregon.gov/DHS/ph/pas/faqs.shtml
Will insurance cover the cost of physician-assisted suicide? Can a patient's family members request physician-assisted suicide on behalf of the patient?

www.compassionandchoices.org
Compassion & Choices Website. The nation's most comprehensive resource for choice in dying. We support, educate and advocate for choice and care at the end…

www.deathwithdignity.org/
Oregon death with dignity-respect the will of the people. Death with dignity became an end-of-life care option in 1994 with the popular passage of the…

www.togopeacefully.com/
This is the definitive website to find data-based answers to questions and concerns people have about hastening death when terminally ill.

www.thebody.com/wa/summer98/dignity.html
Death with dignity, at The Body, the complete HIV/AIDS resource.

www.finalexit.org
US nonprofit organization lists aims such as serving people who are suffering from an intolerable condition.

EXPLANATORY NOTES

1. Garret Keizer, "Life Everlasting. The Religious Right and the Right to Die." *Harper's Magazine*, Feb. (2005): 53.

2. John Shelby Spong, Eighth Episcopal Bishop of Newark. "Death: A Friend to be Welcomed, Not an Enemy to be Defeated." Address to the 2003 national convention of End-of-life Choices, San Diego, California, Jan. 10 (2003).

3. Unrelieved pain is an uncommon reason given by patients who seek aid in dying. The most common reasons are: other physical symptoms, loss of control over bodily functions, wanting to be in control of the process of dying, not wanting to be a burden on others, loss of meaning, loss of dignity, and personal goals (being "ready to die"). See: T. E. Quill and C. K Cassel, "Professional Organizations' Positions Statement on Physician-Assisted Suicide: A Case for Studied Neutrality." *Annals Intern Med*. 138 (2003): 208–211; and, L. Ganzini, S.K. Dobscha, R.T. Heintz, and N. Press, "Oregon Physicians' Perceptions of Patients Who Request Assisted Suicide and Their Families." *Journal of Palliative Medicine*. Vol. 6, No. 3, (2003): 381–390.

4. Ibid. Several studies are cited in the articles noted above, in which 2–35% of hospice patients report severe or unbearable

Explanatory Notes

pain during the last week of life. The studies include data on physical symptoms other than pain, such as shortness of breath or nausea.

5. Unfortunately, symptoms such as nausea, vomiting, shortness of breath, and extreme fatigue are harder to ameliorate than is pain.

6. Most of the opposition to anesthesia in England was from Protestant clergy who deemed it a violation of holy scripture. When Calvinist clergy and others objected to Sir James Simpson's use of chloroform to prevent the pain of childbirth, he quoted from the Scriptures to prove that God was the first anesthetist (Genesis, II,21: "And the Lord God caused a deep sleep to fall upon Adam, and he slept."). Today there is very little religious opposition to relief of suffering during life, but for many Christians suffering while dying is seen as a way of sharing the passion of Christ, and as consistent with God's will. See: "Sacred Congregation for the Doctrine of the Faith: Declaration on Euthanasia. III. The Meaning of Suffering for Christians and the Use of Painkillers." According to Christian teaching, however, suffering, especially suffering during the last moments of life, has a special place in God's saving plan; it is "a sharing in Christ's passion and a union with the redeeming sacrifice which He offered in obedience to the Father's will."

7. By common usage, a terminal illness exists when there is no more effective curative treatment for the patient's disease, and the patient has, in best medical judgment, six months or

less to live. This is the criterion used by Medicare for hospice eligibility.

8. "Sacred Congregation for the Doctrine of the Faith: Declaration on Euthanasia. I. The Value of Human Life." Part 3. While the Roman Catholic Church condemns aid in dying, it teaches that "One must clearly distinguish suicide from that sacrifice of one's life whereby for a higher cause, such as God's glory, the salvation of souls or the service of one's brethren, a person offers his or her own life or puts it in danger." This is an example of excluding from suicide—based on a person's condition, or circumstance—the taking of one's own life.

9. Support for Oregon's Death with Dignity Law cuts across faith, gender, and political lines. See: E. D. Stutsman, "Political Strategy and Legal Change," in, *Physician-Assisted Dying. The Case for Palliative Care & Patient Choice*. Ed. by T. E. Quill and M. P. Battin, The Johns Hopkins University Press, Baltimore, (2004): 245,6.

10. See: S. Gusher, "Meddling could haunt politicians in Schiavo case." *Palm Beach Post*, Palm Beach, Florida, June 24 (2005).

11. For further discussion of Oregon patients who have died under the law in that state, see L. Ganzini, "The Oregon Experience," in, *Physician-Assisted Dying. The Case for Palliative Care & Patient Choice*. Ed. By T. E. Quill and M. P. Battin (The Johns Hopkins University Press, Baltimore, 2004): 165–183.

EXPLANATORY NOTES

12. There has long been a charge that HMOs or insurance companies, as well as government plans, would somehow manipulate doctors or hospitals to influence their patients to end their lives. There has never been any evidence of this happening, but opponents of aid in dying have been quick to use the argument, especially in campaigns to defeat state legislation allowing the practice. A joint study by a well-known opponent and a well-known advocate found no evidence that aid in dying would yield cost saving for managed care plans. See: E. J. Emanuel and M. P. Battin, "What are the Potential Cost Savings from Legalizing Physician-Assisted Dying?" *New England Journal of Medicine*, vol. 339, July 16 (1998): 167–172.

13. In the story of *Antigone*, by Sophocles, Antigone explains to her sister why she has to bury her dead brother, under the King's penalty of death for doing it. She says: *It is the dead, not the living, who make the longest demands. We die forever.* While classicists interpret Antigone's act of burying her brother as placing devotion to the gods as above duty to the state, I believe this statement also shows her understanding of the need to reconcile with the dead. In this case, the need was to satisfy her brother's last wish, and that of all honorable Greeks, for burial. Unfulfilled wishes of the dead last forever.

14. The Hippocratic Oath is frequently cited as an example of an existing medical tradition in opposition to abortion and euthanasia. But it is generally accepted that the Oath was not written by Hippocrates, and did not reflect the common practices and beliefs on these subjects at that time, and one

patristic writer of the third century concluded that Hippocrates performed abortions when delivery of an intact child was impossible. See O. Temkin, "The Idea of the Respect for Life in the History of Medicine," in *Respect for Life in Medicine, Philosophy, and the Law*, O. Temkin, W.K., Frankena, and S. H. Kadish (The Johns Hopkins University Press, Baltimore, 1977).

15. Dr. Kubler-Ross identified five psychological stages of dying: denial, anger, bargaining, depression, and acceptance. Dying patients may not progress through all stages, or in the order given. Her work led to greater study of the psychological aspects of dying. See E. Kubler-Ross, *On Death and Dying* (Macmillan, New York, 1969).

16. For further reading on the distinction between grief and depression, see: S. D. Block, "Assessing and Managing Depression in the Terminally Ill Patient." *Annals of Internal Medicine*, 132 (2000): 209–218.

17. A patient's statement of hopelessness is frequently predetermined by his life views, or religion. Consider two patients, women of the same age who both are dying of breast cancer. The first woman considers herself religious, but does not believe in afterlife. She believes that she is nearing the end of the life she loves, with no chance for recovery. She expresses her grief from dying as "having no hope," and is classified as "depressed." The second woman, also religious, anticipates the joys of redemption and afterlife, and is judged to be not depressed. The difference between the two patients is in the

meanings they give to their impending deaths, and is not a matter of mental health or illness.

18. The question of whether depression in terminally ill patients is a treatable cause of the wish to die has been widely studied and debated in the medical literature. See: M.D. Sullivan, L. Ganzini, and S.J. Younger. "Should Psychiatrists Serve as Gatekeepers for Assisted Dying?" *Hastings Center Report*, July-August (1998): 24–31; L. Ganzini, M.A. Lee, R.T. Heintz, J.D. Bloom, and D.S. Fenn, "The Effect of Depression Treatment on Elderly Patients' Preferences for Life-sustaining Medical Therapy." *Amer. J. Psychiatry*, 151:11 (1994): 1631–36; A.J. Bharucha, R.A. Pearlman, A.L. Back, J.R. Gordon, H. Starks, and C. Hsu, Clarissa. "The Pursuit of Assisted Dying: Role of Psychiatric Factors." *Journal of Palliative Medicine*, 873:6 (2003), R.A. Pearlman, C. Hsu, H. Starks, et al. "Motivations for Assisted Dying: Patient and Family Voices." *Journal of General Internal Medicine*, In Press.

19. Since implementation of the Oregon Death with Dignity Act in late 1997, the Oregon Department of Human Services has issued an annual report regarding usage under the law. See online document available at: www.oregon.gov/DHS/ph/pas.

20. During the second Oregon vote on the Death with Dignity Act, opponents of legalizing aid in dying said that the new law would lead to a decrease in the quality of palliative care generally. One of the best measures of quality of care is the percent participation of dying patients in hospice plans. Since implementation of the law there has been a marked increase in usage of hospices by dying patients in Oregon,

and Oregon now leads the nation in general hospice use. See: B. Coombs, "Model Integrating Assisted Dying with Excellent End-of-Life Care," in, *Physician-Assisted Dying. The Case for Palliative Care & Patient Choice.* Ed. by T. E. Quill and M. P. Battin (The Johns Hopkins University Press, Baltimore, 2004), 190–201.

21. *Merriam-Webster's Collegiate Dictionary, Eleventh Edition*, (Merriam-Webster, Springfield, MA, 2003). See also, www.m-w.com.

22. For further reading, see: D.W. Amundsen, *Medicine, Society, and Faith in the Ancient and Modern Worlds,* (The Johns Hopkins University Press, Baltimore, 1996), and: O. Temkin, "The Idea of the Respect for Life in the History of Medicine." In, *Respect for Life in Medicine, Philosophy, and the Law,* O. Temkin, W.K. Frankena, and S.H. Kadish, (The Johns Hopkins University Press, Baltimore, 1977).

23. "Everything in nature loves and protects itself. Suicide is contrary to natural law…The passage from this life to another and happier one is subject not to man's free will but to the power of God." T. Aquinas, *Summa Theologiae*, (Question 94 of the Prima Secundae).

24. In his address of March 20, 2004, to an international congress, Pope John Paul said, "The sick person in a vegetative state, awaiting recovery or a natural end…" The statement implies that the natural end has not yet occurred for a patient in a vegetative state, even if the vegetative state is of many years. See: Address of John Paul II to the Participants in the International Congress of "Life-Sustaining Treatments and

EXPLANATORY NOTES

Vegetative State: Scientific Advances and Ethical Dilemmas." Saturday, 20 March, 2004. The need to sanctify life "to its natural end" comes out often in Catholic teaching. In an op-ed piece, Carles J. Chaput, the archbishop of Denver, wrote: "If we believe in the sanctity of life from conception to natural death, we need to prove that by our actions, including our political choices." See: "Faith and Patriotism," *New York Times*, (OP-ED, Oct. 22, 2004): A23.

25. In 2004, at a time when Terri Schiavo was still alive but in a persistent vegetative state, Pope John Paul II addressed a group meeting to discuss issues pertaining to vegetative states: Address of John Paul II to the Participants in the International Congress of "Life-Sustaining Treatments and Vegetative State: Scientific Advances and Ethical Dilemmas," (Saturday, 20 March, 2004). Note how, in the title of his talk, the word "persistent" is omitted before "vegetative state." In his remarks, the pope said, "…there is no different diagnosis that corresponds to such a definition, but only a convenient prognostic judgment, relative to the fact that the recovery of patients, statistically speaking, is ever more difficult as the condition of vegetative state is prolonged in time." This reflects his position that prognosis is always uncertain.

26. Daniel Callahan, an opponent of aid in dying, says that the sanctity of life principle has been seduced by technology: "Many of those who would uphold the sanctity of life seem now to believe that they must follow technology wherever it goes so long as it preserves life. Medical technology, the child

of the Enlightenment, has co-opted the ancient principle of sanctity of life and turned it into its handmaiden." I would point out that people, not technology, have been seduced into co-opting the sanctity of life principle. See: D. Callahan, *"The Sanctity of Life Seduced: A Symposium on Medical Ethics,"* The Hastings Center, Garrison, N.Y., (2004).

27. Voluntarily stopping eating and drinking has received a lot of attention as a means of dying for terminally ill patients. Many "end-of-life" experts promote voluntarily stopping eating and drinking as an alternative to other ways of hastening death. There is a growing literature on the subject, primarily in medical/nursing publications. In general, when patients adhere to having no food or water, death comes more quickly and peacefully. When they take small amounts of food or water the end is delayed and less peaceful. Supplemental morphine or other medicine to relieve symptoms is important. My mother, who died 23 days after becoming unable to swallow, did ingest small amounts of fluids for the first 7–10 days; in addition, she was well nourished and hydrated before becoming unable to swallow. The patient's condition before voluntarily stopping eating and drinking, and adherence to refusing all food and liquid, are the two major determinants of time until death. See: L. Ganzini, E.R.Goy, L.R. Miller, et al. "Nurses' Experience with Hospice Patients Who Refuse Food and Fluids to Hasten Death," *New England Journal of Medicine*, 394;4 July 24, (2003): 359–365.

28. Normal skin is turgor is caused by the fluid content of blood vessels, capillaries, and cells. When a body has no fluid

intake, it maintains blood volume by removing water from skin and other organs that are not critical to maintaining blood pressure, and the skin loses its usual fullness.

29. In 1957 a group of doctors asked Pope Pius XII: "Is the suppression of pain and consciousness by the use of narcotics…permitted by religion and morality to the doctor and the patient (even at the approach of death and if one foresees that the use of narcotics will shorten life)?" The Pope answered: "If no other means exist, and if, in the given circumstances, this does not prevent the carrying out of other religious and moral duties: Yes". Pius XII, *Address* of 24 February, 1957; AAS 49, (1957): 147.

30. This procedure was initially called "terminal" sedation, because it was the terminal event, or treatment. Many medical workers did not like the connotation of terminal, which might indicate intent to terminate the patient. Consequently, the procedure now is most commonly called "palliative sedation," or "continuous sedation." It is a good example of semantic change to frame a medical procedure more acceptably.

31. The legal defense of palliative sedation rests on saying that the physician does it to relieve pain, and has no intention to end life. But the cause and effect of the procedure and the patient's death are so evident that many physicians will not do it because they consider it to be euthanasia. See: D. Orentlicher, "The Supreme Court and Physician-Assisted Suicide. Rejecting Assisted Suicide but Embracing Euthanasia," *New England Journal of Medicine*, 337;17, (1997): 1236–39.

32. S. Bachrach, "In the Name of Public Health—Nazi Racial Hygiene," *New England Journal of Medicine*, 351;5, (2004): 417–420.

33. At debates or in casual discussions of aid in dying, opponents invariably evoke the issue of "Nazi euthanasia." Since some forms of physician aid in dying (e.g., withdrawing a life-sustaining feeding tube or ventilator) are often called "passive" euthanasia, the specter of euthanasia hangs over most attempts to help terminally ill patients die peacefully. See: C.R. Browning, *The Origins of the Final Solution*, (University of Nebraska Press/Yad Vashem, Lincoln, (2004). See also, A.I. Batavia, "Disability and Assisted Dying." In, *Physician-Assisted Dying. The Case for Palliative Care & Patient Choice*. Ed. by T. E. Quill and M. P. Battin (The Johns Hopkins University Press, Baltimore, 2004): 59.

34. The association of aid in dying with the word euthanasia is direct and open in The Netherlands, where *voluntary* euthanasia is legal, and so called. If the citizens of any country were overly sensitive to the use of the word euthanasia, it should be especially so in The Netherlands where the Nazi crimes were great. But the Dutch maintain the distinction between voluntary euthanasia, in which the patient of free will requests to die, and the Nazi form of involuntary euthanasia in which a person is put to death involuntarily, or without consent.

35. Most people dying in hospitals could be kept alive for hours or days longer, using all available life support. In the last few days of life many patients lose competence to make medical

decisions and someone, commonly a relative, makes the decision to stop life-sustaining treatments. K. Faber-Langendon, and P.N. Lanken, "Dying Patients in the Intensive Care Unit: Forgoing Treatment, Maintaining Care," *Annals of Internal Medicine*, (2000;133:886–893); and, see also: D. Blymire, "Experts: Living Will Necessary but not Enough," *Carlisle Sentinel*, PA, Aug. 10, (2005); also available online at: www.cumberlink.com/articles/2005/08/10/news/news07.txt.

36. Supreme Court of the United States, Washington et al v. Glucksberg et al. No. 96–110, at 32. 1997.

37. Supreme Court of the United States, No. 96–110 and 95–1858, at 14, 1997.

38. Over the last 25 years, a majority or plurality of adults in the United States has supported a legal means of helping terminally ill patient die, as with aid in dying. See: *Harris Poll*, April 27, 2005: 67% of adults "would like their states to allow Oregon-style aid in dying for terminally ill patients;" *TIME* magazine poll, March, 2005: 52% of Americans said they "agree with the Oregon law," vs. 41% who did not (*TIME*, March 28, 2005); *CBSNews.com*, New York, Nov. 24, 2004, "Poll: Physician-Assisted Suicide:" Should Physician-Assisted Suicide be allowed?" Yes 46%, no 45%.

39. For an overview of some of the propositions that obstruct a religious understanding of dying, see: J.S. Spong, "Death: A Friend to be Welcomed Not an Enemy to be Defeated." An address to the 2003 national convention of *End-of-Life Choices*, San Diego, CA., Jan. 10, 2003.

40. During the seven years' experience in Oregon, approximately 2% of dying patients formally requested lethal prescriptions under the law, physicians granted the request in about 1 in 6 cases, and approximately 64% used the lethal medicine to die. Thus, approximately 10.5% of patients who requested a lethal prescription received and used it to die. About 1.0 per 1,000 of all patients who died in Oregon did so under the law. The number of total deaths under the Death with Dignity Act has slowly risen over the seven years, from 16 in the first year, 1998, to 37 in 2004 (down from 42 in 2003). These data do not suggest the emergence of a policy promoting aid in dying. See: S.W. Tolle, V.P. Tilden, L.L. Drach, et al. *Characteristics and Proportion of Dying Oregonians who Personally Consider Physician-Assisted Suicide. Journal of Clinical Ethics*, 15;2, Summer, (2004):111–119; and, L. Ganzini, H.D. Nelson, T.A. Schmidt, et al. "Physicians' Experiences with the Oregon Death With Dignity Act," *New England Journal of Medicine*, 342 (2000); 557–563; and, S. Okie, "Physician-Assisted Suicide—Oregon and Beyond." *New England Journal of Medicine*, 352;16 (2005): 1627–30. See also, on-line document available at: www.oregon.gov/DHS/ph/pas.

41. The opposition of the organization "Not Dead Yet" has been very vocal, with demonstrations well timed for media attention. However, the majority of disabled people do not oppose aid in dying. See: "Disability and Assisted Dying," A. I. Batavia, *New England Journal of Medicine*, 336 (1997): 1671–73. See also, "AUTONOMY Responds to National

EXPLANATORY NOTES

Council on Disability's Opposition to Oregon Law Legalizing Physician Assisted Dying," at: www.prnewswire.com/cgi-bin/stories.pl?ACCT= 104& STORY=/www/story/11-22-2005/0004221368&EDATE=

42. Statement is based on reports of the Oregon Health Department. Anecdotal evidence suggests that up to half of patients who obtain lethal medicines either die from their diseases before deciding to take the medicine, or decide against this form of death.

43. In support of this opinion, Chief Justice Rehnquist cited American Medical Association statements: *American Medical Association, Code of Ethics* 2.211 (1994), Council on Ethical and Judicial Affairs, and, *Decisions Near the End of Life*, 267 *Journal of the American Medical Association* (1992): 2229, 2233. Cited in: Supreme Court of the United States. No. 95–1858, June 26, 1997.

44. The citations noted by Chief Justice Rehnquist, ibid, are of statements from the executive branch of the American Medical Association. But a survey of AMA members showed that the statements are not representative of the AMA membership. See S.N. Whitney, B.W. Brown, H. Brody, et al. "Views of United States Physicians and Members of the American Medical Association house of Delegates on Physician Assisted-Suicide," *Journal of General Internal Medicine*, 16 (2001): 290–296.

45. See ibid, and, *Business Wire*, 03-03 (2005), "US. Poll: Majority of Doctors Support Ethics of Physician-Assisted Suicide; Plurality Support Legalization of Controversial

Practice," on-line at: www.home.businesswire.com; and, J.S. Cohen, S.D. Fihn, E.J. Boyko, A.R. Jonsen, and R.W. Wood, "Attitudes toward Assisted Suicide and Euthanasia among Physicians in Washington State," *New England Journal of Medicine*, 331 (1994): 89–94; and J.G. Bachman, K.H. Alcser, M.J. Doukas, R.L. Lichtenstein, et al., "Attitudes of Michigan Physicians and the Public Toward Legalizing Assisted Dying and Voluntary Euthanasia," *New England Journal of Medicine*, 334 (1996): 303–309.

46. The citation given in the decision is of testimony of Dr. Leon Kass, a known opponent of "assisted suicide," who testified: "The patient's trust in the doctor's wholehearted devotion to his best interests will be hard to sustain." *Assisted Suicide in the United States*, Hearing before the Subcommittee on the Judiciary, 104th Cong., 2nd Sess., 355–356 (1996).

47. Justice Stevens, concurring, in: Supreme Court of the United States. Nos. 96–110 and 95–1858, June 26, 1997.

48. As noted, physicians prefer to practice privately. While a majority or plurality of U.S. physicians think a physician should be able to help a patient die if there is a compelling humanitarian reason to do so, many are not willing to help in this way so long as the law and the medical societies do not approve of it. On the other hand, physicians know well the possibilities of suffering while dying, and wish to be able to control their own dying. See: T.A. Preston, "Professional Norms and Physician Attitudes Toward Euthanasia," *Journal of Law, Medicine & Ethics*. 22:1, Spring, (1994): 36–40; and, T.D. Kinsella, and M.J. Verhoef, "Determinants of Canadian

Physicians' Opinions about Legaliized Physician-Assisted Suicide: A National Survey," *Annals Royal College of Physicians and Surgeons of Canada*, 32, June, (1999); 211-a.

49. Justice Souter, Washington v. Glucksberg, No. 96–110, 1997, U.S.LEXIS 4039, June 26, 1997.

50. S.N. Whitney, B.W. Brown, H. Brody, et al. "Views of United States Physicians and Members of the American Medical Association house of Delegates on Physician Assisted-Suicide," *Journal General Internal Medicine*, 16 (2001): 290–296.

51. J.G. Bachman, K.H. Alcser, M.J. Doukas, R.L. Lichtenstein, et al, "Attitudes of Michigan Physicians and the Public Toward Legalizing Assisted Dying and Voluntary Euthanasia," *New England Journal of Medicine*, 334 (1996): 303–309.

52. In practice, "morphine drips" for dying patients are not regulated. By personal observations I have never seen a patient or a patient's surrogate decision-maker give informed consent for the treatment before it led to death of the patient, although I have not seen it done for any but patients in the last throes of dying, and have always felt it was done for the benefit of the patient. It sometimes is given temporarily as "routine care," to aid recovery of patients who have had surgery, and not commonly viewed by physicians as a procedure requiring consent. See: T.A. Preston, "Killing Pain, Ending Life," *The New York Times*, OP-ED, Nov. 1, (1994): A15.

53. S.B. Nuland, "The Principle of Hope," *The New Republic*, May 27, (2002).

54. Pickering, John H. "The Continuing Debate over Active Euthanasia." *Bioethics Bulletin,*.3;2, (1994):1.

55. Charles McKhann, a surgeon at Yale University, writes: "Another way of looking at laws that are not universally accepted is to recognize a legal double standard, with laws that apply to some but not to others. The few who break the law do so privately and secretly, not only to avoid detection but to allow the myth of the formal law to be protected. See: C.F. McKhann, *A Time to Die,* (Yale University Press, New Haven, 1999: 221).

56. *When Death is Sought: Assisted Dying and Euthanasia in the Medical Context.* (New York State Task Force on Life and the Law; 1994):163).

57. Vacco v. Quill, No. 95–1858, 1997 U.S. LEXIS 4038 (June 26, 1997), pg 15.

58. G.J. Annas, "Death by Prescription-The Oregon Initiative." *New England Journal of Medicine,* 331(1994):1240-43; and, G.J. Annas, "The Promised End-Constitutional Aspects of Assisted Dying," *New England Journal of Medicine,* 335, (1996): 683–87.

59. There are numerous anecdotal reports of patients who would or might have used violent means to end their lives, had they not had the security of a means to die with medication. See: T.A. Preston, and R. Mero, "Observations Concerning Terminally Ill Patients Who Choose Suicide," in, M.P. Battin, and A.G. Lipman, ed, *Drug Use in Assisted Dying and Euthanasia,* (Pharmaceutical Products Press, Binghamton, NY, 1996): 182–92.

EXPLANATORY NOTES

60. David Orentlicher, of the Center of Law and Health at Indiana University, testified before the U.S. House Judiciary Committee regarding a proposed "Pain Relief Promotion Act" that would put prescription of narcotics under federal oversight and control: "No matter how many words you attempt to write into this act...the reality...is that doctors would rather avoid risk, interrogation, and investigation at all costs."

61. Under this proposal, the law would stipulate the requirements necessary for a physician to have immunity under the law. The requirements would in general follow the example of the Oregon statute. See: J.A. Tulsky, A. Alpers, and B. Lo, "A Middle Ground on Physician-Assisted Suicide," *Cambridge Quarterly of Healthcare Ethics*, (1995): 33–43.

62. A specific proposal along these lines, "The Patients' Choice and Comfort Act," or PCCA, was developed in Arizona as a compromise for possible future legislation. The PCCA, or legislation similar to it, would allow a patient to obtain lethal medicines if diagnosed as terminally ill by his attending physician and a consulting physician. A limitation of the PCCA is the requirement that a patient request the medication by an advance directive *before* becoming terminally ill, or, if already terminally ill, at least six months prior to acting under the PCCA. Since many patients die less than six months after knowledge of being terminally ill, this provision in effect means a patient must have an advance directive asking for the provisions of the PCCA in place before becoming terminally ill.

Patient-Directed Dying

This provision of the PCCA is intended to prevent abuse by restricting its use to patients who have long-held views on wanting aid in dying if necessary, and by prohibiting it for those who might be coerced during the later stages of dying. Fewer patients could avail themselves of this approach than are eligible under the law in Oregon, but it would have the advantage of forcing people to plan in advance how they want to die, and would be less susceptible to charges of abuse. However, it has the disadvantage of excluding patients who, for whatever reason, do not have an advance directive prior to becoming terminally ill. The PCCA is just one example of how an "affirmative" legal defense might operate. The requirement of an advance directive prior to terminal illness need not be present in other "affirmative" legal defense laws.

63. Sophocles expressed similar sentiments. See, for example, *Oepidus at Colonus*, Choral Poem at end of Scene V:

Though he has watched a decent age pass by,
A man will sometimes still desire the world.
I swear I see no wisdom in that man.
The endless hours pile up a drift of pain
More unrelieved each day; and as for pleasure,
When he is sunken in excessive age,
You will not see his pleasure anywhere.

INDEX

A
Absolutism, 70
Abuse, disabled persons, 118
Active euthanasia, 143
Adamant family opposition, 70-71
Afterlife, 28
Aid in dying, defined, 143
American Medical Association, 124-125, 168, 170
Annas, George, 131
Antidepressants, 42, 64. *See also* Depression
Antisuicide laws, 120-122
Appetite loss, 78-81
Aquinas, Saint Thomas, 74
Artificial respirators, 100-102
Assisted dying, defined, 143

C
Catholic Church (Catholicism), 25, 27, 29, 157, 162
Chemotherapy, 16, 26, 43-45, 55-56, 74, 90, 121-122
Clark, Barney, 10
Clinical depression, 63, 65, 143

Index

Coerced aid in dying, 134
Comfort care, 19, 56, 122, 125, 140, 144-146
Congestive heart failure, 61, 83
Criminal charges, 134
Culture of death, 115
Curative treatment, 55, 156
Curing *vs.* caring, 54

D
Death, defined, 144
Dehydration, 79, 96
Depression, 42, 63-65, 118, 140, 143, 147, 159-160
Disabled persons, abuse of, 118
Divine law, 72
Do Not Rescuscitate orders, 106. *See also* Living Will
Double effect principle, 92, 132, 144
Dying
   existential reasons for, 21
   future of, 134-137
   process of, 4-5

E
Eating and drinking, termination of, 78-86
Emotional shock of fatal diagnosis, 42-43
Enabling dying patient, 24-25
Eugenics movement, 97
Euthanasia, 25, 73, 93-98, 134, 139, 143-144, 146-147, 149, 151, 156-158, 164-165, 169-171

F

Family approval and objections, 30-31, 33, 37-40, 66-70, 68, 104
Fatigue and dying, 20
Feeding tubes, 51, 75, 101-104, 165
Financial factors, 30-34

G

Glucksberg, 124, 126, 131, 166, 170
God's will, 20
Grief, 26, 64, 67, 151-152, 159

H

Hastened dying, 19, 28, 33, 69, 144-145, 153, 163
Health plans, 32
Hippocratic concepts, 47
Hippocratic Oath, 129, 158
Hitler, Adolf, 97-98
HMOs, 32-33, 158
Home-hospice plan, 90
Hopelessness, 63-64
Hospice care, 19, 33, 35-40, 57, 64, 68, 80-81, 90, 93, 99, 106, 116, 122, 124, 140, 145-147, 151, 155-157, 160-161, 163

I

Insurance, 30-33, 152, 153, 158
Integrity, 21, 125-126
In vitro fertilization, 74

Index

J
Judeo-Christian teachings, 73

K
"Killing" concept, misconceptions regarding, 71-72
Kubler-Ross, Elizabeth, 63

L
Legal issues, 115-127
Legal profession, 129-130
Legislation, 126-127
Living Will, 5, 10, 104, 106, 111, 166

M
Mechanical respiration, 100-101, 107
Medicaid, 32-33
Medical insurance, 31-32
Medically managed dying, 47
Medical recommendations, 50
Medical technology, 46, 76
Medicare, 32-33
Medicine by the book, 50
Meeting dying patients, 17
Morphine use, 20, 37, 40, 79, 81-82, 84, 89-90, 92-95, 99-101, 104, 110, 121
128, 132, 144-145, 163, 170

N
Natural death, 47-48
"Natural law" concept, 74-76
Nazi Germany, 96-98
Needless suffering, prolonging, 11, 54
Nuland, Sherwin, 128

O
Oregon Death With Dignity Act, 29, 32, 64, 115, 117-118, 124, 126-127, 133, 139-141, 152-153, 157, 160-161, 166-168, 171-173
Orthodox Jews, 29

P
Palliative care, 19-20, 22, 32, 43, 54, 64-65, 118, 124, 131, 133, 145-146, 150-151, 157, 160-161, 165
Palliative sedation, 95-96
Panic reaction, 63
Panic response, 42-43
Passive euthanasia, 146
Patient abandonment, 38-39
Patient-directed dying, defined, 146
Patient's Choice and Comfort Act, 172
Physician-assisted suicide, 147
Physician-enabled dying, 146-147
Physicians
    central involvement in dying, 49-50
    controlling dying process and, 94-95
    curing *vs.* caring, 54

insistence on treating to very end, 54-55
views on legislation, 128
views on patient self-determination, 52
withdrawal from dying patients, 55
Pope John Paul II, 75
Prescriptions, lethal, 30-32, 56-57, 61, 68, 71, 77, 92, 95, 99, 101-102, 116, 119-120, 132, 139, 141, 143, 167, 172
Privatization, 127-134
Public-health measures, 44-45

R
Redemption and damnation, 28
Religious beliefs, 27-28, 68, 100, 136
Respirator, artificial, 100-101
Right-to-die advocacy organizations, 57

S
Sanctity of life concept, 72, 73-74, 75-77, 135-136, 147, 162-163
Schiavo, Terri, 75
Sedation, palliative, 95-96, 104, 119-120
Sense of purpose, 21
Situational depression, 64, 143, 147
"Slow euthanasia," 95
Social eugenics, 97
Special-interest groups, 126
Spiritual suffering, 22
State laws, changing, 126-127
State's interest, 120-124

Stopping treatments, 103-104
Suffering
  spiritual value in, 21
  unnecessary, 20
  varying views on, 20-21
Suicide, 23-27, 71, 73, 114, 116, 119-122, 124, 127, 129, 132, 134, 143, 146-147, 147, 149-150, 152-153, 155, 157, 161, 162, 166-172

T
Terminal illness, 49, 63, 67, 122-124, 134, 136, 139, 151, 156, 173
Terminally ill, defined, 147

U
U.S. Justice Department, 132
U.S. Supreme Court, 120-122, 124-127, 131

V
Vegetative state, 75
Verifiable exceptions, allowing, 133

W
Washington v. Glucksberg, 124
"Will of God," 48
Withdrawal, physician, 55

To order copies of *Patient-Directed Dying*
see the bookstore at iUniverse.com
http://www.iuniverse.com/bookstore/index.asp
Orders can be placed online or by phone
For more information contact
the iUniverse Book Order Department at
1-800-288-4677 ext. 501
or by email at
book.orders@iuniverse.com

978-1-58348-461-6
1-58348-461-2

www.ingramcontent.com/pod-product-compliance
Lightning Source LLC
Chambersburg PA
CBHW021541200526
45163CB00014B/556